KV-190-274

Japanese-Led Companies

UNDERSTANDING HOW TO MAKE THEM
YOUR CUSTOMERS

SERIES EDITOR
BARRIE DALE
UMIST

Japanese-Led Companies

UNDERSTANDING HOW TO MAKE THEM YOUR CUSTOMERS

Nigel Holden and Matt Burgess

McGRAW-HILL BOOK COMPANY

London · New York · St Louis · San Francisco · Auckland · Bogotá
Caracas · Lisbon · Madrid · Mexico · Milan · Montreal
New Delhi · Panama · Paris · San Juan · São Paulo
Singapore · Sydney · Tokyo · Toronto

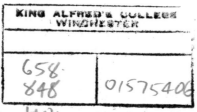

658.
848

01575406

Published by   HUL
McGRAW-HILL Book Company Europe
Shoppenhangers Road, Maidenhead, Berkshire SL6 2QL, England
Telephone: 0628 23432
Fax: 0628 770224

British Library Cataloguing in Publication Data
Holden, Nigel
  Japanese-led Companies: Understanding How to Make Them Your
  Customers. –
  (McGraw-Hill Quality in Action Series)
  I. Title II. Burgess, Matt III. Series
  658.800952

  ISBN 0-07-707817-9

Library of Congress Cataloging-in-Publication Data
Holden, Nigel
  Japanese-led companies: understanding how to make them your customers /
  Nigel Holden and Matt Burgess.
     p. cm. -- (McGraw-Hill quality in action series)
  Includes bibliographical references and index.
  ISBN 0-07-707817-9
  1. Export marketing--Great Britain--Management. 2. Great Britain--
  Commerce--Japan. 3. Japan--Commerce--Great Britain. 4. Corporations,
  Japanese--Management. 5. Corporate culture--Japan. 6. Consumer
  behavior--Japan.   I. Burgess, Matt.   II. Title.   III. Series.
  HF1416.6.G7H64   1994
  658.8'48--dc20   93-37640
                                                                  CIP

Copyright © 1994 McGraw-Hill International (UK) Limited.
All rights reserved. No part of this publication may be reproduced, stored in a retrieval
system, or transmitted, in any form or by any means, electronic, mechanical,
photocopying, recording, or otherwise, without the prior permission of McGraw-Hill
International (UK) Limited.

1234 CUP 97654

Typeset by Hybert Design & Type, Maidenhead, Berkshire SL6 4JP.
Printed and bound in Great Britain at the University Press, Cambridge.

Contents

Foreword

Japan represents a very strong competitive threat to the industries of the Western world. However, it also represents an opportunity. As Japanese companies establish themselves throughout the world, they provide outlets for would-be suppliers. In addition, Japanese industry and commerce if only because of the trade imbalance are encouraged by their government to purchase from abroad.

It is particularly unfortunate that, for a whole range of reasons, most Western companies see Japan as an impossible market to penetrate and Japanese companies based in their own markets difficult to supply. My own experience has shown that the difficulties are real but that with a proper understanding of Japanese ways of working a lasting and profitable business is possible.

This book is a perceptive guide to prospective suppliers to Japanese companies, both because of its methodology but also because of its recognition of the differences between Japanese companies at home and abroad. Its case studies show a range of situations with which many Western companies will identify. Its lessons are well worth learning, even if difficult to apply. When I chaired a JEBA (Japan Electronic Business Association) briefing session at which Dr Nigel Holden outlined some of the practical messages derived from this book, I was struck by how much these accorded, not only with my own experience at Mullard and Remploy, but also with those of the other companies in the audience who had been successful in their own businesses with Japanese industry.

The book cannot guarantee success to those that read it but it can provide them with a means of proper preparation for what will be a long process in which perseverance will be rewarded in the end. In essence, the Japanese approach to business is different from that elsewhere but it has been successful. All companies must try to understand the needs of their customers, as indeed, buyers should understand their suppliers. Indeed, as the Japanese abroad begin to resemble their Western counterparts, perhaps someone will write a book to help Japanese managers to understand how to deal with industry outside Japan. Not everything done in the West is wrong.

Sir Ivor Cohen,
Chairman,
Japan Electronic Business Association (JEBA)*

---

* JEBA is an association of companies based in Britain, committed to increase the sale of British-made components to Japanese electronic companies. It is industry-led but supported by the Department of Trade and Industry.

Preface

As this book is a joint effort, it will be helpful to explain how it came to be written. During 1990 and 1991 Holden happened to be supervising the research projects of two students who, independently of each other, were making detailed empirical studies of business relationships involving UK firms as suppliers to Japanese industrial customers. One student, Morten Abrahamsen, was preparing an MSc thesis investigating the impact of cultural and psychological factors on long-term relationships between UK suppliers of industrial products — from heavy capital equipment to mechanical components — to customers in Japan. The other student, Matt Burgess, was looking at interactions of UK subcontractors supplying a variety of component types to major Japanese OEMs (original equipment manufacturers) in the UK.

Morten Abrahamsen and Matt Burgess both made use of the same conceptual model for investigating relationships between buyers and suppliers of industrial goods. This model, associated with an international consortium of marketing scholars known as the IMP (International Marketing and Purchasing) Group, has been very fruitfully applied to investigate the interactions of industrial suppliers and buyers in a European context. The studies of Abrahamsen and Burgess represent the very first attempt to use it to describe the UK-Japanese interactions in detail. Although both projects differed in scale, research focus and methodology, they both dealt with one main theme: relationship management involving a cross-section of UK firms supplying technical goods and Japanese industrial customers.

Thus, Abrahamsen and Burgess were involved in gathering and analysing data on these relationships along complementary (and ultimately mutually enriching) lines. But more than that, they were both unearthing revelatory information on the nature of UK-Japanese business interactions involving the supply of technical goods. All this information, and the implications to be drawn from it, seemed far too important to be consigned to a university library. Holden's task as chief editor was to harmonize and integrate the two studies, relate them to existing knowledge about business development with Japan, and eventually transform the whole text into a book for a business readership.

Acknowledgements

This book is primarily the work of Holden and Burgess, who wish to express warm appreciation to the Great Britain-Sasakawa Foundation and the United Distillers Company for generous financial support which made both projects possible. We also gratefully acknowledge the assistance of the managers and their firms who gave up so much of their valuable time to relate so candidly their experiences of dealing with Japanese companies.

Introduction

> In the academic world there is a discipline devoted to the study of interpersonal relationships. To my knowledge, however, not one scholar specialises in the study of *inter-company* relationships. This is a serious omission. We need to know much more than we do about what makes effective corporate relationships work.
>
> Kennichi Omae, *The borderless world* (1990).

WHY THIS BOOK IS DIFFERENT

The contributions by Western marketing commentators on Japan, in its domestic and international contexts, have been fairly extensive. Broadly speaking, Western marketing writers have concentrated their attention on three main topics: the penetration — or rather the relative non-penetration — of the Japanese market by Western firms; the impact of cultural factors on Japanese marketing behaviour; and Japanese global marketing, which has tended to be viewed from the point of view of corporate strategy.

This book is different from many books on doing business with Japan because it begins where most leave off. It is commonplace for practically every book or article on business with Japan to stress the importance of developing a long-term business relationship with Japanese counterparts. But none seems to spell out what managing relationships with Japanese customers entails for firms, their managers and that all important group of people who are their firms' 'Japan-interfacers'.

This book also recognizes that the development of a long-term relationship with Japanese customers needs what is called 'cultural sensitivity'. Everyone knows that firms must be culturally sensitive with Japanese business counterparts; but not so many people understand exactly what this sensitivity entails. It is a good deal more than knowing that business cards are *de rigueur*; or that one must pay considerable attention to how Japanese businessmen seat themselves around the negotiation table; or that there is a large language problem. The key thing is to understand the impact of cultural differences and perceptual mismatches on how Japanese business partners understand *you*. This book is an attempt to address these issues by means of case studies, that examine how a cross-section of UK firms, all supplying industrial or technical products, handle relationships with their Japanese customers, whether based in the UK or in Japan. Not everything will apply to you, but a lot will. The first set of case studies – on the export relationships – are prefaced by two chapters. The first one is of a general introductory nature.

The second goes into some detail about a conceptual framework for analysing and understanding cross-cultural interactions with Japanese customers. This conceptual framework derives from extensive researches by a multicountry team of marketing scholars focusing on transnational buyer-seller relationships involving the exchange of industrial goods. The reader is asked not to skip the second chapter on the grounds that it is 'too theoretical', for without these explanations the ability to understand the two sets of case studies with all the accompanying commentary and analysis will be largely nullified. In other words, the reader will miss out on the very benefits for which this book may have been purchased!

One cannot approach a complex business culture such as the Japanese one using minimal concepts or by perpetuating the same misinformed myths about Japan and the Japanese. No one who reads all of this book should be in any doubt about why 'atmosphere' – a topic which will receive a good deal of attention – is so crucial a concept in managing relationships with Japanese customers. Even better for the business reader, there are guidelines on what attaining a conducive business atmosphere actually entails. How you speak, dress and hand over your business card are all elements to examine from a new perspective.

WHO SHOULD READ THIS BOOK?

In the first instance this book is aimed at managers who, in a variety of firms, are suppliers of industrial goods and technical services to Japanese customers based in the UK and in Japan itself. Through the commentary, case studies and analysis, it should help this general cross-section of managers gain insights into handling relationships with those customers. It should throw light on some hitherto baffling examples of Japanese behaviour, and give pointers about modifying the future marketing and selling approach.

It is, however, very likely that the book will appeal to a much wider readership of business practitioners engaged in marketing quite separate product lines to Japanese customers. For example, agencies who are actively trying to attract Japanese investment into their regions may discover that the book has some important messages for them; likewise those who are seeking to persuade UK-based Japanese firms to purchase so-called prestige locations, or a range of financial or legal services, may find this book will be of value to them. Firms concerned with marketing to Japan proper may find this book more perceptive than the proverbial dos and don'ts of doing business in Japan. In short, this book is really for anyone who knows that the essence of doing business with Japanese customers is all about relationships, but for whom the actual management of these relationships is either a mystery or, as yet, one of the great unlearned arts of modern business.

A WORD ON THE STRUCTURE OF THIS BOOK

The book comprises nine chapters, and is divided into four self-contained sections. Chapters 1 and 2 form the introductory section: Chapter 1 reviews the current state of management and marketing writing on Japan, and Chapter 2 describes the conceptual model and related approach for investigating and analysing UK–Japanese industrial interactions. Chapters 3 and 4 constitute the second distinctive section, focusing on the case studies prepared by Abrahamsen on the impact of cultural and psychological factors on the development of long-term relationships involving five UK industrial suppliers and their customers in Japan.

The next self-contained section, Chapters 5, 6 and 7, focuses on the studies made by Burgess on the relationships between five suppliers of automotive, mechanical and electronic components to UK-based Japanese manufacturers. The last section comprises Chapters 8 and 9: Chapter 8 attempts to synthesize the findings of the two main studies, and Chapter 9 suggests pointers for companies and their 'Japan-interfacers' on how to improve the quality of their business interactions with Japanese customers, suggesting some unconventional approaches to marketing strategy – and tactics.

PART

1

CHAPTER
1

Japanese customers: the gods and guests of the marketing playground

---

A person learns rhetoric and good breeding along with the language, for nobody can know Japanese without knowing how he must address the great and the lowly, the nobles and the commoners, and the decorum to be observed with them all.
Lourenco Mexia, SJ (1540–1599). Quoted in: Michael Cooper, *They came to Japan* (1981).

The Japanese, like the Athenians of old, have always hankered after some new thing.
C.R. Boxer, *The Christian century in Japan 1549–1650* (1974).

JAPAN: THE NEVER-ENDING EXPLOSION OF ENERGY

For more than a decade writers and commentators on Japanese business and management have been groping for explanation and enlightenment to account for Japan's phenomenal rise to economic and technological pre-eminence. As they weigh up a variety of factors, the Japanese economy continues to be in a state of continuous overdrive, rising above the recession and paralysis which are affecting all other industrial nations so harshly. The sheer power of the Japanese economy is well illustrated by the following facts and figures.

Japan produces one quarter of the world's passenger cars, has the world's largest merchant fleet, and by the mid-1980s that Japanese industry was using up to 70 per cent of the world's production of robots (Kotler et al, 1986). The first seven biggest banks in the world in terms of assets and deposits are Japanese. Japan's total foreign investment in 1989 was $68 000m, a 1200 per cent increase over 1979. Of all industrialized countries, Japan has the least unemployment and the lowest rate of inflation (source: Keizai Koho Center, 1990). These statistics read well for a country that has been described as 'a resource-starved fringe of scraggly islands off the east coast ... of Eurasia' (Reischauer, 1984).

Additionally, Japan continues to spend about three per cent of its national income on R&D, proportionally more than the USA or Germany (Anglo-Japanese Economic Institute, 1991). Japanese management practice, no matter how poorly understood in other countries, has become a universal byword for innovation, product quality, excellence in manufacturing and harmonious industrial relations. In the UK, which is the major European location of off-shore Japanese manufacturing, the Japanese influence has been so profound that management scholars now speak of 'the Japanization of British industry'. All this bears out the simple truth that Japan 'one way or the other, is affecting everybody's lives' (Emmott, 1990). Not that the Japanese influence is confined to the economic sphere, as never before in history, the outside world is exposed to Japanese culture and values.

The outside world is exposed to Japanese people more than at any time in the past: not only do more foreigners live and work in Japan, but more and more Japanese visit or reside in other countries. In 1989 nearly 600 000 Japanese lived or worked abroad and nearly 10 millions travelled abroad on holiday, a third of them heading for the USA (Keizai Koho Center,

1991). Some 30 000 Japanese live in the UK, many connected with Japan's 140 manufacturing operations. Yet, despite this unprecedented contact, Japan remains at best an object of 'sceptical admiration' (Emmott, 1990), sometimes turning to awe, sometimes to irritated wariness, even hostility.

A major element of this sceptical admiration is a general Western uncertainty about unfathoming Japan and its role in the modern world. This is aggravated by a Japanese tendency to claim to be misunderstood, without sending out clear messages to compensate. The Japanese put the resulting confusions, antagonisms and even hostility down to unbridgeable cultural differences between themselves and the rest of mankind. What, however, may not be appreciated so readily is that the Japanese are inclined to use cultural difference as a form of special pleading. The well-informed Dutch journalist, Karel van Wolferen (1989), has commented on this phenomenon, observing: 'Government officials demonstrate great conviction that all their actions and everything Japan is responsible for internationally can be explained by Japanese culture *and must therefore be excused*' (our emphasis). As van Wolferen further notes: 'Explaining Japan to the world has spawned a formidable sub-industry of writing and publishing'.

JAPAN AS PORTRAYED IN MANAGEMENT LITERATURE

It is hardly surprising therefore that management writing on Japan has long been preoccupied with the culture-specific nature of Japanese management philosophies and practices. Some years ago Western management literature was almost panic-driven to find 'the secrets of Japanese success'; the Japanese salaryman (corporation executive) was portrayed, largely against the facts of history, as a kind of reincarnated samurai warrior; the Japanese, having poised themselves 'at the cutting edge of management and technology' (Dower, 1985), were seen to be about to take over the world. In short, we were exhorted to learn from Japan. In recent years a noticeably less excitable quality is infusing Western management writing. These days, thankfully, the dominant question is no longer concerned with *what* the Japanese are doing – the question that caused the panic – but *why* are they doing it that way.

This means that, to some degree, the Western tradition (extending back more than one hundred years) of alternating between completely underestimating Japan and according Japan superman status is at long last being superseded by more balanced accounts of Japan's business behaviour. Several authors come to mind: Abbeglen and Stalk (1985) on the nature of Japanese corporations; Ronald Dore (1986) on various aspects of Japanese industrialism; Bill Emmott (1990) on the new, wealthy Japan; and Mark Zimmerman on the sociocultural context of Japanese business activities (1985). These and others have performed a valuable service by avoiding the intimidating interrogative 'what' in order to concentrate on 'why', which invites probing and reflection. Given this general and welcome change to enlightenment, how for their part do marketing writers approach Japan? The answer is: in a haphazard way.

A BRIEF REVIEW OF WESTERN MARKETING LITERATURE ON JAPAN

There is a very considerable literature on marketing to Japan and marketing by Japanese organizations, with contributions from both Japanese and non-Japanese: academic writers, journalists, management consultants, diplomats, government officials, gurus, apologists and so forth. But this literature is diffuse, multipolar, uneven, ephemeral, and, of course, rapidly expanding. One of the major branches of marketing literature concerns the so-called penetration of the Japanese market. This literature can be broken down into four broad areas relating to 1) formal barriers to market entry; 2) informal barriers to market entry; 3) descriptions of the distribution system with emphasis on the retail sector; and 4) a wide range of material in case-study format, some of it commissioned by Japanese official agencies, which highlights instances of Western firms successfully doing business in Japan (*'pour encourager les autres'* is the subliminal theme of this writing).

Much ink, type-writer ribbon and mega-bytes of PC memory have been expended on the issue of penetration of the Japanese market by foreign firms. It is an issue which has created the notorious 'trade friction' between Japan and the USA, and Japan and the EC, and it is not easy to separate questions of marketing to Japan from wrangles over Japan's huge trade surpluses and frequent Western recriminations over Japanese protectionism. The vexation and recrimination have reached such a pitch that Mme Cresson, the former Prime Minister of France, declared in her earlier capacity as Minister for Foreign Affairs: 'It is clear that Japan is an adversary that does not play by the rules and has an absolute desire to conquer the world.' And she adds pungently: 'You have to be naive or blind not to recognize this' (*The Economist*, 18 May 1991). This, to the Japanese, is Japan-bashing of the worst possible kind (so much for the commemorations of the French Revolution in Tokyo's magnificent department stores in 1987, gloriously promoted as one of the grand events of *Japanese* history!).

The former French Prime Minister is no doubt mindful of the occasion when a French supplier of skis found its products being rejected by the Japanese customs authorities on the extraordinary grounds that Japanese snow is different from French snow. Similarly, certain US meat products were banned from Japan on the pretext that they were not suitable for 'unique' Japanese intestines. It is in the USA, of course, where Mme Cresson's outburst strikes responsive chords.

The USA is by far the biggest recipient of Japan's overseas direct investment - nearly $33 000m in 1989 (Keizai Koho Center, 1990). But while enormous sums of Japanese money create new jobs for hundreds of Americans, promote regional development, and support welfare programmes and academic endeavour, the mighty yen is also buying property as well as companies that have − or rather had − revered institutional status in the USA. Thus, when Matsushita, the world's biggest electronics company, took over Universal Studios in 1990, it was seen as more than a business deal: Japan was buying up Hollywood. Similar resentment surfaced later when Sony bought RCA, one of the great show-biz names, and the Rockefeller Center in New York. Moreover, after years of careful study, the Japanese have begun to perfect that most advantageous of corporate arts: how to work the

US political lobbying system.

At the same time, the perception remained that American products were simply not getting into the Japanese market, no matter how much the Japanese Government and its agencies could demonstrate with portfolios of statistics how liberalized and open to foreign products the Japanese market had become. The distribution system, the most frequently invoked non-tariff barrier, militates against foreign efforts to penetrate the Japanese market. Quite apart from the natural instinct of the armies of small independent retail traders to be patriotic in their purchases, these same businesses insist on frequent but small deliveries and a high level of personalized service. But there is a consolation: the whole system is so 'regulated', not to say rigged, that even new Japanese entrants are discriminated against!

The endless wrangles have led Japan and the USA to the brink of trade wars on more than one occasion, and Japan's cautious stand over the Gulf War in 1991 will only fuel American convictions that Japan's global business is protected by US political and military power. A recent addition to the welter of books on US–Japanese trade friction had the ominous title, *The coming war between Japan and the US*. It is a sobering thought that *The Economist's* reviewer found the scenario plausible.

But to keep formal barriers separate from informal ones is an artificial exercise. The Japanese have a long-standing tendency to justify formal barriers with reference to cultural (i.e. nationalistic) considerations. This has prompted various authors to emphasize that the Japanese *culture* or the Japanese perception of their own 'uniqueness' represent the greatest obstacle to Western–Japanese interactions. According to Best (1990), 'many Western executives still don't realize that succeeding in Japan is far more dependent on a company's ability to recognize and adapt to the cultural differences between Japan and the West'. Zimmerman (1985) reminds us that the Japanese 'are not on our wave-length'. The matter is neatly summed up by Robert Sharp of the American Chamber of Commerce in Tokyo: 'The fundamental causes of our trade frictions with Japan lie in the interplay between different histories, cultures and national politics' (in: Sullivan, 1986).

In tackling the knotty matter of cultural differences, it is possible to classify marketing writing into three general areas, which lay stress on various desirable corporate and personal attributes for coping with Japan. These areas are: 1) sensitivity to cultural differences; 2) the paramountcy of personal relationships and the related need to develop these in the long term on the basis of mutual trust; and 3) dealing with the Japanese, including negotiation.

The literature on cultural issues and marketing falls into two main complementary camps: 'know your enemy' and 'when in Rome, do as the Romans do'. Strictly speaking, the second is not an entirely felicitous description of the writing concerned, at least if it is taken too literally. A culturally-sensitive rendering of the well-known adage would be: 'when in Japan, do not behave like an uncivilized barbarian'. Either way, the guiding principle of this subset of literature, exemplified by Artzt (1989), Elmashmawi (1990) and Zimmerman (1985), is that awareness of cultural differences and a preparedness to understand Japanese cultural values in relation to Western (i.e. US) cultural values represent the path to enlightenment. But, according to a Japanese author, Namiki (1988), the alleged inaccessibility of the Japanese market is all to do with misperceptions, many of which are peddled by the Western mass media bent on 'Japan-bashing'.

Concerning the paramountcy of personal relationships, virtually every article and book on how to do business with Japan stresses this point. For example, a recent book with the title *Cracking the Japanese market* puts relationship development at the top of its suggested four-prong strategy for addressing the Japanese market. It advises:

> The operation should be designed to begin and support a close relationship between your company and your Japanese customers. This means that it must provide an avenue for feedback so that continuous product and process improvements can be made. It should also provide a means for establishing future requirements for products and services, allow for mutually beneficial joint development efforts, and create an environment of intertwined destinies with the customers (Morgan and Morgan, 1991).

But one does not read quite so much, in this or other offerings, on precisely *how* these relationships come about, how they are sustained, or how commitment and trust develop. This section of writing is both platitudinous and weak on what Japanese firms expect or require of these much-vaunted personal relationships. Writers who think they are illuminating the reader about the impact of cultural differences have a nasty habit of not understanding Japanese psychology. For example, Moyle (1985) tells us that the single greatest challenge for the foreign party in negotiating a Japanese joint venture is to 'appreciate the amount of time and energy which the negotiation process will require'. Everyone knows that negotiating a joint venture is going to be time-consuming; the greatest challenge has more to do with fielding astute personnel who are not merely patient negotiators, but over several months are also able to eschew signs of vexation or impatience. Graham and Sano (1986), in their study of US-Japanese negotiations, seem to think that 'ideally, American negotiators should speak fluent Japanese'. But this misses the crucially important point (dealt with in chapter 4) that the Japanese are wary of foreigners with a very good command of Japanese: they can be unneeded cultural intruders.

This brings us appropriately to the matter of dealing with the Japanese. This subset of the literature is connected with two interrelated topics: communication with the Japanese, including negotiation, and the Japanese penchant for so-called non-verbal communication. The major contributions on negotiating with the Japanese are by American scholars (e.g. Graham, 1983; Graham, 1985; Graham and Sano, 1984, 1986; Graham and Andrews, 1987; Tung, 1984).

Graham and his colleagues are mainly concerned with negotiation as a process. Negotiations are viewed as episodes (with clear-cut stages in some instances) concerned with achieving a specific business objective. These and other authors have studiously avoided seeing negotiation as a form of relationship management, possibly leading to long-term involvements and commitments. This, it could be argued, misses the psychological reality of negotiations or business discussions from the Japanese point of view.

Although this book is not explicitly concerned with negotiation, it is concerned with relationship formation between UK suppliers and Japanese customers. It will, therefore, have something to say on negotiation as a total process of inter-organizational bonding without, incidentally, suggesting that there are clear-cut stages. The only thing that is clear-cut is that dealing with Japanese businessmen requires insights into the workings of the 'Japanese business mind'.

These American contributions, not for the first time with respect to cross-cultural issues, tell us more about American preferences and practices than those of the highlighted partner. What is curious about the American contributions on negotiation is that they are weak on the role of language in Western – Japanese negotiations, yet some extremely enlightening contributions on Japanese language and communication difficulties have appeared in US management literature (e.g. Gibney, Zimmerman). It is curious that the authors on negotiation have not turned to this body of literature for insights.

We are therefore forced to the conclusion that marketing literature on doing business in Japan is certainly plentiful, but varied in quality and insight. It is perhaps worth spelling out precisely those factors which strongly inhibit understanding of Japanese marketing behaviour – and purchasing behaviour – in their own socio-cultural context:

- The well-established tendency to impose Western constructs and models on Japanese behaviour rather than studying Japanese behaviour in its own right.
- The intractable nature of the language barrier which 1) serves as a highly complex intensifier of perceptual mismatches; and 2) seals off Western management researchers, as a universal fraternity, from Japanese-language material and the Japanese Weltanschauung ('world-view').
- Marketing writers' tendencies to underrate or misconceive the nature of the 'clash and fusion' of Japanese civilization with Western cultures since the middle of the last century.
- An absence of empirical studies on the implementation of Japanese marketing management decisions (though there is no shortage of material theorizing about Japanese marketing strategy).

In the light of the above factors we can make some conclusions about the general quality and orientation of the current Western marketing literature on Japan. Five issues stand out.

1 Marketing writers do not pay specific attention to the problems of marketing industrial goods (i.e. technical products). Those studies which touch on the marketing of technical products, whether in terms of export relationships (e.g. JETRO, 1984 and 1990) or sub-contractor relationships (e.g. Trevor and Christie, 1988), do so without reference to a guiding conceptual framework. Although there is a growing literature on the development of sub-contractor relationships with Japanese manufacturers based in the UK and other EC countries, this too is general and descriptive.

2 Although various authors stress the Japanese preference for long-term business relationships, the organizational and management implications for Western suppliers are rarely discussed.

3 The question of the impact of culture is treated in a non-systematic way, and, related to this, not enough emphasis is placed on the Japanese national psychology with specific reference to the acute Japanese sense of difference from non-Japanese.

4 Culture is artificially separated from language issues: it is generally not grasped that the Japanese language is 'the most remarkable of all the identifiable constellations of Japanese social and cultural behaviour patterns' (Miller, 1977), and its role as an intensifier of perceptual mismatches is correspondingly underplayed.

5 A further limitation of this literature is that it is primarily concerned with penetrating the Japanese market, which is treated as an abstract entity rather than as a locale of flesh-and-blood customers.

The above points are a direct challenge to all marketing authors, including ourselves. As stated in the introduction, the focus of this book is relationship development with Japanese industrial customers. Before looking at relationships proper, it is of exceptional importance to understand, and not forget, what the word *customer* means in the Japanese context.

CUSTOMER WORSHIP

The theme of this book is an exploration of relationship development between UK industrial firms and their Japanese customers. Although many of these customers are enormously powerful organizations and are indeed world-leaders in their class, it is advisable to have a clear idea of what the word 'customer' evokes and implies in Japanese culture. We shall begin then with a brief explanation of the Japanese word for 'customer' from linguistic, social and historical perspectives. There is no point in discussing customer relationships in any Japanese context, whether these involve solely Japanese partners or Japanese and non-Japanese partners, until the Japanese concept of the customer is grasped.

It is well-known that in Japan 'the customer is god' (O-kyaku-sama wa kami-sama desu). Its adulatory tone immediately suggests that this well-known aphorism does not correlate culturally with the Western maxim, 'the customer is king'. Many Western writers on doing business in Japan are quick to latch onto this divine status in a bid to remind foreign firms that Japanese customers expect the highest imaginable levels of service and attention. But the most telling part of the Japanese maxim centres on the meaning of the word 'customer'. In Japanese, the word is 'o-kyaku-sama'. The semantic essence is in 'kyuaku', whose generic meaning is, not customer, but *guest*. In other words, customer is a derived meaning from the word guest. The particles 'o-' and 'sama' are both honorific forms; the first particle is usually translated into English, in a somewhat stilted way, as honourable. The second particle is a very polite form, virtually impossible to translate by a single word, but it has the flavour of 'much respected one(s)' or perhaps 'gracious one(s)'.

This incursion into Japanese linguistics is important, for now we know that customers are not only divine in Japan, their patronage also does great honour to a purveyor of goods or services. This patronage does not necessarily imply that customers have to buy anything; their mere presence on the premises of the establishment concerned is sufficient to accord them shimmering courtesies and respectful bows – even if, in the end, they decline to purchase anything. From this we may deduce that how customers or 'honourable guests' are addressed is of extreme importance to any kind of shop, service organization or company. The practice, of course, goes to the very heart of Japanese social organization and the centuries-long preference for harmonious interaction, entailing manifestations of respect for one's elders and betters, and a readiness to be of service to anyone where socially appropriate (an important qualification).

In line with these traditions and values, all self-respecting organizations provide their staff with training in what is called 'business etiquette': a learned body of wisdom about appropriate conduct *vis-à-vis* customers (and *vis-à-vis* superiors.) New recruits will learn how to bow, how to sit properly (and where to sit at meetings), how to present business cards, how to store business cards received, how to speak to customers both on the telephone and in personal encounters, how to be appropriately attired for business, how to write business letters and so on.

Female staff (often university graduates) will be trained as receptionists in the intellectually undemanding, yet socially crucially important role of welcoming 'honourable guests'. Telephonists will virtually learn a new language, acquiring a new, high-pitched voice in the process ('Who is calling, please?' takes on new dimensions of solicitous politeness in the Japanese language). Female staff, too, will learn how to conduct visitors to the discussion room: how to enter it, how to serve tea to the visitors and participants, and how to leave the room without disturbing anyone. Major companies sometimes employ former JAL hostesses as trainers.

Staff in shops, especially the leading department stores, learn how to receive money from a customer and how to return the change with all the necessary polite language, and they spend hours practising that most beautiful of the commercial arts – folding paper and packaging things for customers.

To sum up so far: Japanese companies do everything in their power to ensure that the 'honourable guest' gets and retains a favourable impression through direct and indirect contact with them. This is part of the service to which 'honourable guests', by virtue of their exalted status, are automatically entitled. Japanese companies continually try to maintain and improve the quality of contact and communication with customers in exactly the same way they are concerned to steadfastly improve products to secure customer satisfaction. One more point, easily overlooked from a Western perspective: it is always stressed to the Japanese how important it is to learn about their customers and learn how to deal with them on the basis of accumulated wisdom.

JAPAN AS A MARKETING PLAYGROUND

It can surely be no coincidence that the business practice we call marketing was already practised in a recognizably modern form in sixteenth-century Japan, almost exactly 100 years before the American War of Independence. It is worth quoting this extract from no less an authority than Peter Drucker (1973), who regards Japanese as the first people to grasp the marketing concept (the notion that customer satisfaction is central to business success):

> Marketing was invented in Japan around 1650 [writes Drucker] by the first member of the Mitsui family to settle in Tokyo as a merchant and to open what might be called the first department store. He anticipated by a full 250 years basic Sears, Roebuck policies: to be the buyer for the customers, to design the right products for them, and to develop sources for their production; the principle of money back and no questions asked; and the idea of offering a large assortment of products to his customers rather than focusing on a craft, a product category, or a process.

By the end of the nineteenth century, after some forty or fifty years' exposure to Westernizing influences, Tokyo had two leading department stores. One was the renowned Mitsukoshi store (the one that Drucker alluded to), which still sets the tone in Japan; the other was called Shirokiya. An old silk store, Shirokiya became the first shop in Japan to stock and sell Western clothes; and, as if to underline Japan's tradition of placing the latest technology at the service of its customers, it had one of the first telephones in Tokyo 'which, however, was kept out of sight, in a stairwell, lest it disturb people' (Seidensticker, 1983). An intense rivalry sprang up between the two stores, and they sought to outdo each other by another familiar Japanese marketing practice: using 'bold new innovations' (Seidensticker, 1983) to attract and keep customers. Mitsukoshi may have been behind Shirokiya in grasping the significance of the telephone, but it was 'better at advertising and "image-making"'; and, 'though purveying almost everything to almost everyone, it has preserved a certain air of doing so with elegance' (Seidensticker, 1983). When after the turn of the century Mitsukoshi first added a second floor with show-cases, 'these innovations were so startling that they were for a long time resisted'.

The very location of the stores was a spur to competition. They stood directly opposite each other in the middle of Tokyo near a bridge 'to which all roads led'. They not only attracted customers through innovation and exotic (i.e. European and American) merchandise, they also provided culture and entertainment in bigger and better equipped premises. Around 1908, for example, Shirokiya installed a games room and 'exhibition halls that give the modern Japanese department store certain aspects of a museum and amusement park' (Seidensticker, 1983). By around the same time the department stores, in Tokyo at least, had forced the decline of bazaars as the leading shopping attractions. Mitsukoshi, Shirokiya and the like 'finally emerged as a playground for the whole family, on whatever level of society' (Seidensticker, 1983).

We do not need to continue this brief history of Japanese retailing. Its development before the First World War clearly bore all the hallmarks of Japanese-style marketing and customer development: intense rivalry to secure not just the customers' money, but also their attention and favour; the use of new technology (in the nineteenth century, the telephone and advertising) to improve direct communication with new and potential customers; the making of business a pleasure for customers, whose other tastes may be indulged while an 'honourable guest' of the retailer. We scarcely need add that products were of the highest standards, service of an impeccable order. What is more, these same ideals concerning product quality and service were already being imbued in Japan's burgeoning light and heavy industries of the late nineteenth century, as well as in the growing banking sector. For example, the first ever company motto of Nippon Electric Limited (NEC), founded in 1898, one of the world's leading electronics companies was: 'Better products, better services' (NEC, 1984).

Taking up a word used in a previous paragraph, it is by no means outlandish to suggest that it is restrictive to see Japan as a market; perhaps the once-named topsy-turvey land is more aptly described as a *marketing playground*, a complex terrain of business, culture, general revelry and scandal all too often involving, and sometimes bringing low, the high and mighty. Customers are the gods and guests of Japan's marketing playground.

MORE THOUGHTS ABOUT THE RATIONALE OF THIS BOOK

The purpose of delving into points about Japanese history and social interaction is to set the scene for the later examinations of the interactions involving Japanese customers and UK suppliers. Specifically it has been the intention to convey something of the psychological world in which Japanese customers are 'worshipped' by Japanese companies. This brief incursion into such a complex aspect of contemporary life in Japan is necessary because one of the aims of this book is to explore the nature of cultural differences and perceptual mismatches when UK firms attempt to develop relationships with Japanese customers.

Unlike hosts of other books and articles on doing business with Japan, we are not concerned with 'how to penetrate the Japanese market'; nor are we directly concerned with the formulation and implementation of marketing strategies as such. Furthermore, we have practically nothing to say on promotion or advertising, and we deal fleetingly with the distribution system. Instead we focus on a topic that is much mentioned, yet seldom systematically tackled: the development of long-term relationships with Japanese customers. Just as it is well-known that 'the customer is god' in Japan, so everyone knows of the Japanese preference to develop long-term relationships with customers on a close, sometimes intense, personal basis.

But, when the (would-be) supplier is not Japanese, the psychological world of the Japanese customer undergoes transformations. The following quotation from Zimmerman (1985), which we will discuss at some length in a later chapter, neatly sums up this transformation: 'When a Westerner meets a Japanese, many factors contribute to a sense of mutual unease. Each has his or her prejudices to overcome, and there is a cultural gap so wide that many Westerners do not even know it is there'.

This book is concerned with exploring the nature of this cultural gap between Japanese customers and a group of UK suppliers. The approach, however, is somewhat unusual and it is important to explain the rationale. First, when we talk of Japanese customers, we do not have in mind a vague generality: we are focusing specifically on Japanese purchasers of technical and industrial goods who are buying either on their own account or for an end-user further down the supply chain. This means then that we are focusing on the marketing of industrial goods, items which are used in the Japanese customers' or the Japanese end-users' own productive systems.

To guide our explorations we shall make use of a conceptual model for investigating buyer – seller relationships in industrial markets. The advantage of this model, and the research procedure associated with it, is that it has been developed on the basis of transnational interactions and has evolved concepts for handling the impact of culture on buyer – seller relationships. This approach is explained in Chapter 2.

As noted in the Introduction, we are going to examine two sets of relationships with Japanese industrial customers. In Chapters 3 and 4 we will examine and analyse the perceptions and experiences of five UK firms in their interactions with their customers in Japan. The companies concerned are suppliers of heavy electrical plant, sound systems, industrial chemicals and components for the paper industry. Then, in Chapters 5, 6 and 7 there will be corresponding treatment of the interactions of five different UK firms whose customers are UK-based manufacturing subsidiaries of major Japanese corporations involved in the production of cars, electronics products and agricultural equipment. In Chapter 8 we will attempt to compare and contrast the differing nature of cultural and perceptual mismatches involving the two sets of Japanese customers. On the basis of the experiences recorded in earlier chapters, we produce a general model, showing phases through which a Western company must pass in order to achieve the status of trusted supplier. It is hoped that this model, for which the information of all the preceding chapters is essential reading, will provide insights to UK industrial firms developing business relationships with Japanese customers, wherever these customers are.

Industrial interactions: culture, distance and atmosphere

All things considered, the would-be critic of Japanese mind, manners, and morals has a thankless task before him.
Basil Hall Chamberlain, *Japanese things* (1904/1982).

Like many American writers in Japan I felt no overt resistance, just a constant undertow that seemed to work against me.
David Halberstam, *The reckoning* (1986).

In the introduction and in the preceding chapter great emphasis was placed on the fact that the core of this book is concerned with UK suppliers of technical goods to Japanese industrial customers in the home country or established in the UK. For readers with an interest in UK business with Japan, but without any general knowledge of marketing or of industrial marketing in particular, the emphasis on Japanese industrial customers appears for highly specific reasons. This requires a brief excursion into general theories of, and assumptions about, marketing behaviour. Without this 'deviation', the relevance of the IMP approach and related model will lose some crucial significance for the way in which we analyse our informants' involvements with Japanese customers.

Until around 20 years ago marketing scholars paid very little attention to the nature of selling and purchasing industrial products. Although it was clear that in industrial markets customers were, generally speaking, manufacturers who purchased and used industrial goods and services to sustain and improve their own productive efficiency, marketing scholars were inclined to describe the buying and selling arrangements as somehow related to the more familiar and far more researched field of consumer marketing. It was not until the early 1970s that some real breakthroughs occurred, when some American scholars produced models of industrial (and organizational) buyer behaviour, which stressed how this kind of buying − professional, collective, rational − differed from consumer buying behaviour. The models of industrial/organizational buyer behaviour, associated with Webster and Wind (1972) and Sheth (1973), though not reproduced here, tended to focus on the seller, who was represented as the proactive party influencing a so-called buying centre. Thus, although these American scholars undoubtedly advanced a general conceptual understanding of the rather distinctive nature of industrial − as opposed to consumer − buying and selling, they unwittingly reinforced the prevailing view of industrial marketing which suggested that it still largely conformed to the classic marketing mix assumptions about marketing. This meant that the marketplace behaviour of suppliers of heavy electrical equipment, machine tools, roller-bearings and so forth was assumed to be generally understandable in terms of manipulation of the four key marketing mix elements which affected product policy (i.e., what to make and for whom, pricing, promotion, and distribution arrangements).

But this 'cosy' view of industrial marketing was soon to be revised. First, a group of economists, who became known as the 'New Institutionalists', began to propagate ideas that actors in the marketplace did not just buy and sell things to each other; they invested in each other as buyers and sellers. To be more precise, they invested in those relationships which tended to guarantee longer-term security and reliability of business. These ideas were taken up, in the mid 1970s, by a group of marketing scholars from the University of Manchester and the University of Uppsala in Sweden, who had become critical of the still-prevailing influence of the marketing mix approach to industrial marketing, the emphasis on discrete purchases, and the lesser role ascribed to the purchasing function.

The Manchester and Uppsala marketing scholars were joined by sympathetic colleagues from business schools and management departments in France, Germany and Italy, eventually forming a multicountry research consortium which became known as the IMP Group, i.e. the International Marketing and Purchasing Group. As of 1975 the IMP Group began to make empirical studies of buyer-seller interactions in industrial markets involving firms from the five European countries. The thoroughness of the empirical investigations necessitated continual improvement of the research approach and data-gathering techniques.

By the early 1980s some 1200 transnational buyer-seller relationships had been studied. So it was that the IMP Group developed new procedures for the investigation, description and analysis of buyer-seller interactions in industrial markets. Known as the 'Interaction Approach', these procedures were primarily concerned with the focal relationship between buyers and sellers, and the impact on this relationship of a wide range of environmental and organizational influences.

THE INTERACTION APPROACH

The IMP Group argue that conventional approaches to industrial marketing, with their emphasis on 1) discrete purchasing decisions as the basis for exchange and 2) manipulation of the marketing mix as the basis for marketing strategy, do not reflect the characteristics of purchase and supply in industrial markets. The starting-point for the Interaction Approach can be summarized as follows.

First, both buyers and sellers are active participants in the market, with each party actively being engaged in sounding out suitable partners. Previous studies, by focusing on selling organizations as the more dynamic participants, tended to overlook the fact that buyers, too, actively seek suppliers.

Second, the IMP Group established that the relationship between buyer and seller 'is frequently long-term, close and involving a complex pattern of interaction between and within each company' (Ford, 1990). In fact, buyers and sellers may be more preoccupied with maintaining and managing these relationships than with making straightforward purchases or sales.

Third, links between buyers and sellers in industrial markets may become institutionalized into a set of roles, and the parties expect each other to behave according to these roles. Such practices may be formalized in written agreements and are often underpinned by informal arrangements. Thus, involvements in relationships of this kind require both parties to adapt to each other's way of working. Mutual adaptation is a form of cooperation, but one which may entail conflicts which in turn can place relationships under some strain. Fourth, the Interaction Approach acknowledges that certain classes of industrial products, such as capital plant, are purchased infrequently and, as such, cannot be seen as part of a continuous product exchange.

On the basis of its very extensive empirical investigations, the IMP group has developed a model (see Fig. 2.1), known as the Interaction Model, to describe the relationships between buyers and seller in industrial markets (Håkansson, 1982). It is this model which is going to be used in subsequent chapters to provide the framework for investigating the interactions involving UK suppliers of technical goods with Japanese industrial customers. For this reason it is important to explain the 'logic' of the model and to introduce some of the terminology that goes with it. After the general explanation, there will be a short discussion of attempts to use the model to describe Japanese industrial marketing and purchasing behaviour. The chapter will then conclude by highlighting one particular element of the model that will act as an anchor for directing investigation of the UK-Japanese interactions.

According to the Interaction Approach there are four core variables

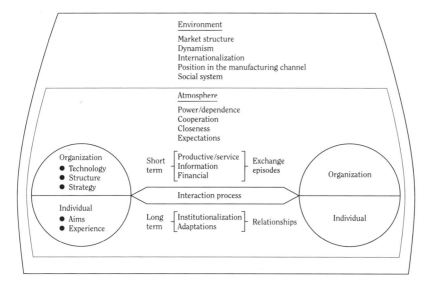

FIGURE 2.1   Main Elements of the Interaction Model

Source: H. Håkansson (ed.), *International Marketing & Purchasing of Industrial Goods*, John Wiley, 1982.

that influence the conduct of relationships between the participants in the market: the process of interaction; the interacting parties; the environment in which interaction takes place; and the atmosphere affecting and affected by the interaction. One of the key points about the model and the underlying Interaction Approach is that we are not just concerned with an analysis of these groups of variables, but also with the relationships between them.

THE INTERACTION PROCESS

The key point about the interaction process is that product and other exchanges are said to take place in terms of single *episodes*, but after some time, exchange episodes develop into a *relationship*. The IMP Group recognize four interdependent types of exchange: 1) product or service exchange,

2) information exchange, 3) financial exchange, and 4) social exchange. Each type of exchange processes is considered briefly.

Product or service exchange

This type of exchange is often the core of the relationship, evolving around the exchange of products and services. Consequently, the conduct of this exchange process can exert a very strong influence over the nature of the relationship. A great deal of uncertainty may be connected to product and service exchange. For example, the seller may not be certain whether the product really meets the customer's needs. The customer, on the other hand, may experience uncertainties when purchasing a supplier's products without previous experience.

Information exchange

Information exchange cements interpersonal relationships while being central to the product and service exchange. Provision of desired information to facilitate product exchanges is of considerable importance for clarifying matters pertaining to product installation, use and after-sales service. Without information exchange suppliers are unlikely to obtain full feedback on the performance of their products. Information exchange takes place informally (especially in the context of established relationships) or in accordance with more formal procedures.

Financial exchange

Although the Interaction Approach is not directly concerned with economic analyses of the conduct of relationships, it acknowledges that financial exchange in terms of payments for products delivered will have some effect upon the relationship in terms of uncertainty concerned with currency fluctuations, and perceived risk about the solvency of the other partner.

Social exchange

Social exchange is perhaps the most important factor in reducing need uncertainty between the interacting parties. In brief, need uncertainty refers to suppliers' uncertainty as to how best to satisfy customers in the wider context of their business; correspondingly, buyers may show a lack of appreciation of suppliers' problems in making their products and services available. This is particularly relevant when there exists a linguistic or cultural barrier between the parties. Social exchange episodes help to build up mutual trust and, over time, these put interactions on a more permanent, more mutually-adaptive basis.

As the various exchange episodes become more common, they create conditions for long-term relationships. When partners in long-term relationships have a very good idea of the part each is to play, then it is possible to regard the relationships as institutionalized. In practice, quite specific individual and organizational contact patterns are built up between the two companies and these contact patterns will help facilitate interactions.

THE INTERACTING PARTIES

Interactions between companies in industrial markets do not only depend on exchange; the various attributes of each of the parties involved also bring influence to bear. The IMP Group highlights four 'organization-related' elements: 1) technology; 2) organizational size, structure and strategy; 3) organizational experience; and 4) individuals in the interacting organizations.

Technology

The technology associated with the product being exchanged, both in terms of its manufacture and in terms of its application, becomes a vital factor in cementing the establishment of an inter-organizational relationship. The extent of the 'technological gap' between two interacting companies will exert an influence on the power/dependence ratio between them.

Organizational size, structure and strategy

An organization with considerable resources may be in the position of dominating the other interacting party, particularly if the technology is of a novel kind. In general, a relationship may be supplier-dominated, customer-dominated or characterized by mutual dependence. The nature of relationships will largely depend upon the size, structure and strategy of the parties in question.

Organizational experience
A relationship may be affected by the interacting parties' aggregated experience of similar relationships and their experience with the market.

Individuals
At the heart of every relationship are the transactions between individuals in each company, involving the 'integration' of their different backgrounds, motivation and experiences. Personal relationships are a vital factor in cementing a relationship, involving complex forms of information exchange, mutual assessment, negotiation, adaptive behaviour and crisis management.

THE INTERACTION ENVIRONMENT
Interactions between buyers and sellers in industrial markets take place in a wider context, that of an environment which is perceived as being made up of five elements: 1) market structure; 2) dynamism; 3) internationalization; 4) position in the manufacturing channel; and 5) the social system.

Market structure
Market structure is determined by the concentration of firms in the market, and the associated level of competition in turn determines the characteristics of exchange between a supplier and a customer. The decision to establish a long-term relationship is influenced by the number of possible partners available. In an oligopolist market, for example, the choice of partners may be limited and already existing buyer-seller relationships may act as a barrier to would-be market entrants.

Dynamism
The degree of dynamism within a relationship may exercise an influence

in two opposite ways. On the one hand, close cooperation between the parties reduces need uncertainty and perceived distance between them: this is because both parties can anticipate each others' actions and reactions on the basis of mutual experience. On the other hand, the opportunity costs of relying on a single partner may be considerable.

Internationalization
The degree to which both the buying and selling market is internationalized will also have a great effect on inter-firm relationships. The nature and scope of firms' international involvements as well as their sense of international mission and commitment are crucial determinants in their capacity to set up and manage relationships with foreign customers and business partners.

Position in the manufacturing channel
A company can easily be a supplier, distributor and customer all at the same time, depending on its position within the extended 'channel' from prime manufacturer to end user. The associated interdependencies will influence the company's relationships with other firms in the channel. For example, it may be limited in its relationships to its customers by the delivery capacity of its suppliers.

The social system
The perceptions that parties have of each other may also influence the conduct of a relationship. This is particularly relevant to international marketing, as the interplay of different cultures and value systems exerts a considerable influence over the processes of product exchange and information exchange.

ATMOSPHERE
One of the major influences on relationship formation is 'atmosphere'. Grasping the importance of atmosphere is essential to understanding one of the

key, implicit 'human-relations requirements' that the Japanese *need* in all their involvements with any business partner. The term atmosphere refers to the quality of a buyer-seller relationship derived from experience, which serves in turn as a determinant of expectations about future cooperation. It has been succinctly described by two Swedish researchers as 'the sum of feelings, intentions, will and interest' of business partners and their capacity to trust each other (Hallén and Sandstrom, 1989). Therefore, atmosphere concerns the general nature of a relationship as derived from the aggregated exchange episodes and the routinization of the relationship. But at the same time it is a kind of descriptor of the overall context in which the relationship exists, given the specific characteristics of the parties involved. As such, atmosphere is treated separately from the environment, and for this important reason: whereas the environment may have similar effects on a number of relationships, the atmosphere will differ from one buyer-seller relationship to another.

Thus, atmosphere may be described in terms of the power or dependence existing between the parties, the level of cooperation or conflict that characterizes the relationship, the trust or mistrust existent, the degree of commitment the parties have to their relationship, the degree of mutual understanding versus a large degree of misunderstanding present, and the overall closeness or distance between the parties. Moreover, by its nature atmosphere is a kind of barometer of the trust and expectations which buyers and suppliers bring to their interactions.

It is to be emphasized that the IMP Interaction Model grew out of extensive researches into industrial buying and selling behaviour on a transnational basis. Specifically, the IMP data-base has detailed information on combinations of interactions involving industrial buyers and suppliers from five European countries: France, Germany, Italy, Sweden and the UK. What these data on analysis show perfectly clearly is that firms from each of these countries have reasonably characteristic approaches to their international marketing behaviour and preferences for how they are approached by foreign suppliers. Thus a study of some 300 interactions by Turnbull and Cunningham (1981) found Swedes and British are less likely than Germans and Italians to haggle over prices; that language and culture are serious barriers to entry into the Italian and especially the French market; that the British have a marked preference for exhibiting personal friendliness in their business contacts; that German buyers and other customer staff prize technical and commercial competence in their suppliers; and that Italians are not inclined to be interested in joint product development with their foreign suppliers.

The implication of the Turnbull and Cunningham study is that successful transnational industrial marketing and purchasing as forms of relationship management required different degrees of adaptability and professional competence according to the cultures involved.

The fact that the Interaction Approach was able to tease out certain national tendencies in relation to cross-cultural industrial buying and purchasing as interactive behaviour suggests its suitability for investigating 'new' interacting parties. The IMP model will, of course, be used later in this study to investigate UK-Japanese interactions. But, in passing, it is worth noting that two sets of researchers have used the model about the Japanese marketing style, arguing that the Interaction Approach, with its emphasis on the building of long-term relationships in industrial markets, is an excellent tool for analysing the specific features of Japanese marketing.

Turnbull and Yamada (1984) drew particular attention to the institutionalized relationships between large corporations and small and medium sized companies that are customary in Japan, noting that this kind of 'Interactive Marketing' was a powerful factor in creating Japan's international competitiveness while deterring foreign firms from entering the Japanese market. Failure to understand this 'outsider-shunning' interactive marketing in effect formed a major informal barrier to market entry.

For his part, Holden (1991) discusses Japanese marketing style in terms of the various elements and variables of the Interaction Model, observing that 'the Interaction Approach, which emphasizes empirical, non-normative methodologies, may well provide a satisfactorily flexible framework for studying Japanese buyer-seller behaviour'. But in this case variables have to be reworked or re-perceived in order to take account of the peculiarities of Japanese marketing interactions and distinctive ways of doing business in Japan, involving factors such as the fulfilment of obligations, the preference for stylized behaviour, and the tendency to create business through exploitation of personal networks. Thus the Interaction Approach facilitates the study of potential cultural mismatches and perceptions of intentions that may be an element of Japanese interactions with foreign firms.

Both these attempts to explain Japanese marketing behaviour in terms of the Interaction Model remain theoretical, and it should be noted that their main focus is on buyer-seller relationships *within* Japan. None of the authors is much concerned about the possibilities of exploiting the Interaction Approach for the study of long-term relationships between Japanese and non-Japanese firms. This 'omission', combined with the by now obvious potential of the Interaction Approach in this respect, has paved the way for the two interrelated studies on UK-Japanese interactions in the form of 'export relationships' (Chapters 3 and 4) and 'sub-contractor relationships' (Chapters 5, 6 and 7).

Before proceeding to the practical application of the Interaction Approach, however, we need to refer to one important conceptual element associated with it. This concerns the obverse of the idea of closeness in relationships: namely forms of 'distance'. This refers to a complex set of cultural, social and psychological impediments preventing buyers and sellers from achieving closeness. The closeness/distance aspect of relationships is a facet of atmosphere. It can be said to bind the Interaction Approach directly to points made in Chapter 1 about 'perceptual mismatches', 'communication gaps' and 'misunderstanding' – terms that infuse much of the marketing literature on the nature of business dealings involving Japanese and Western firms. As 'distance' is going to feature a good deal in subsequent chapters, we need to pay careful attention to this useful, though admittedly elusive, concept.

THE CONCEPT OF DISTANCE

In terms of the Interaction Approach the capacity for firms to form relationships, as opposed to do business with each other on a sporadic basis, is linked to a corresponding capacity to achieve closeness. From the seller's point of view closeness refers to an organizational competence which strives to understand customers and their requirements and to anticipate how these will evolve over time. Implied in this view of closeness is that the customer, who after all has a vested interest in securing reliability of supply, also makes available to (chosen) sellers corresponding information about present and future requirements.

Various studies undertaken by members of the IMP Group suggest that the achievement and maintenance of closeness is particularly difficult in cases in which partners have to overcome linguistic, cultural and psychological barriers at the personal and organizational levels of interaction. This, of course, is not to say that firms find it impossible to deal with each other, but the various impediments to closeness create conditions which lead to frictions between the parties. These frictions may take the form of personal antagonisms or may express themselves as managerial exasperation. Holden recalls an instance in which the managing director of a UK high-tech company summed up his attitude to doing business in France with these words: 'I don't know why we bother!'

Working against the achievement of closeness is the corresponding opposing tendency, called 'distance'. This concept refers to the general amalgam of actors, from formal trade barriers to the impact of differing cultural perspectives, inhibiting smooth interactions and arresting relationship development. Closeness, by contrast, seems to refer to an undifferentiated state of mutual understanding and is an altogether more complex term. Although in the marketing literature increasingly distance has been used as a codeword to describe the impact of cultural and psychological constraints on transnational buyer-seller relationships, the term was first associated with geographical distance.

In 1956 Beckerman published an article in which he posited that countries tended to choose neighbouring and other geographically close countries as trading partners in order to minimize transportation costs. In this sense 'geographical distance' was a vital element in market selection. But Beckerman went a step further. He acknowledged that 'apart from the general reduction in economic distances ... a special problem is posed by *psychic distance*' (our emphasis). The reduction of this form of distance depended 'on the extent to which foreign sources have been personally contacted and cultivated'.

Some of these ideas were developed by Håkansson and Wootz (1975), who studied supplier selection in an international context, and found that purchasers tended to select suppliers geographically close to them as a form of uncertainty reduction – 'the better the devil you know' principle. It was then a small step to the realization, explored mainly by Swedish scholars, that cultural affinities and the influence of psychic distance have some impact on the internationalization of firms (Johanson and Wiedersheim-Paul, 1975).

These themes were further developed by Ford (1980) who suggested that firms' evaluations of each other as potential new suppliers and customers are conditioned by three main factors: experience, uncertainty and distance. Ford described distance as having five aspects:

1 *Geographical distance* the physical distance between interacting firms' locations.
2 *Social distance* the extent to which the individuals and organizations in a relationship are familiar with each others' way of working.
3 *Cultural distance* the degree to which the norms, values or working methods between two companies differ because of their separate national characteristics.
4 *Technological distance* the differences between two companies' product and process technologies.
5 *Time distance* the time which must elapse between establishing contact, placing an order, and the actual transfer of the product or service involved.

Ford argued that, unless firms conscientiously reduced the effects of these various distance factors, they could not bring the relationship to the stage known as institutionalization. Ford, who in fact suggests a succession of five stages of distance-reduction from no experience and high uncertainty to commitment and institutionalization, did not specifically deal with Beckerman's notion of psychic distance. But two Swedish scholars, Hallen and Wiedersheim-Paul revived interest in the topic in 1979 and 1984. As it is going to be important in the coming study of UK–Japanese interactions, the concept of psychic distance is dealt with at some length below.

Psychic distance

Hallén and Wiedersheim-Paul (1984) described psychic distance in terms of differences in perceptions between buyer and seller regarding either needs or offers. In fact they saw four kinds of perceptions at work:

- the customer's perception of his own need
- the customer's perception of the supplier's offer
- the supplier's perception of his own offer
- the supplier's perception of the customer's needs.

With these so-called 'perception packages', Hallén and Wiedersheim-Paul (1984) suggested that incongruities between the respective perceptual positions of the buyer and supplier led to a 'marketing gap' – a potentially unbridgeable set of buyer and supplier perceptions about how to best harmonize offers with needs. We do not need to allow this complicated set of double perceptions to detain us, but it does lead to a more robust definition of psychic distance than that offered above. Psychic distance, say the Swedish scholars, relates to 'the difficulty a supplier has to perceive or estimate the needs of a customer *or* the corresponding difficulty a customer experiences in perceiving the supplier's offer'.

Proceeding from there, Hallén and Wiedersheim-Paul suggest that it is possible to envisage psychic distance as made up of three determinants: 1) cultural affinity; 2) trust; and 3) experience.

Cultural affinity

This refers to the degree to which two interacting parties are familiar with the language, business habits, cultural environment, legal environment, etc., of each other. Thus, cultural affinity is an important determinant for firms' ability to estimate the needs and requirements of the other party. High cultural affinity is a major factor reducing psychic distance between two parties, but as Hallén and Johanson (1985) say 'inter-country affinity is not necessarily symmetrical'. Their research established that 'Purchasers in Britain consider the affinity with German suppliers fairly high, whereas the German purchasers find their affinity with British suppliers much lower'.

Trust

Trust is a vital part of a relationship since many arrangements cannot be formalized and depend entirely upon mutual trust. Hallen and Johanson (1985) also concluded that trust was an important factor in reducing psychic distance, and may in many cases offset low cultural affinity.

Experience

Past, present and future experiences of individuals in the interacting organizations exert a direct influence on the level of psychic distance in a relationship in that they reinforce, modify or disconfirm national prejudices and stereotypes. Thus it has been argued that the development of personal relationships is an important means of reducing psychic distance (Cunningham and Homse, 1986).

The relationship between cultural affinity, trust and experience is illustrated in Fig. 2.2.

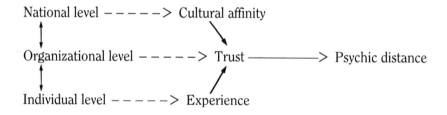

FIGURE 2.2 The relationship between cultural affinity, trust and experience
(Based on Hallén and Wiedersheim-Paul (1984)).

THE RELATIONSHIP BETWEEN CULTURAL, SOCIAL AND PSYCHIC DISTANCE

In contrast to geographical, technological and time distance, the three remaining varieties — social, cultural and psychic — are perceived differences which appear to diminish in intensity with experience. Common sense dictates that this must indeed be the case.

It is tempting to treat these three types of distance as three separate concepts. Nevertheless, even though they may be described separately as the analysis above suggests, the concepts are too interlinked to justify separate treatment. Going back to Ford's (1980) definition of cultural distance ('the degree to which norms, values or working methods between two companies differ because of their separate national characteristics'), and comparing this with Hallén and Wiedersheim-Paul's (1984) definition of cultural affinity ('the perceived impact of cultural similarity in different dimensions such as language, business habits, cultural environment, legal environment, etc.'), it becomes apparent that cultural distance in Ford's (1980) terms and cultural affinity in Hallén and Wiedersheim-Paul's (1984) terms are more or less opposite concepts or, rather, polar extremes on a continuum. This suggests that cultural distance is a major determinant of psychic distance.

Correspondingly, Ford's (1980) definition of social distance ('the extent to which both the individuals and organizations in a relationship are unfamiliar with each others' ways of working'), may be set against Hallén and Wiedersheim-Paul's (1984) description of experience ('individual experience can result in preconceptions regarding suppliers and customers ... These prejudices will affect attitudes and behaviour towards those suppliers and buyers. Individual experiences — past and present — will together form the organizational experience of the firm ... This experience will make the firm more or less suited to establish relations with organizations in certain environments ...'). It is evident that social distance in Ford's (1980) terms and experience in Hallén and Wiedersheim-Paul's (1984) terms are also opposite concepts. Thus, social distance may also be seen as a determinant of psychic distance. We may further note that feelings of trust are associated with cultural affinity and feelings of mistrust with cultural distance.

We are now in a position to produce two simple equations to show the relationship between the three types of distance concepts, using the vital catalysts, trust and mistrust, as determinants of closeness and distance.

1   Cultural distance
    + Mistrust
    + Social distance
    ─────────────────
    = Psychic distance
    ─────────────────

2   Cultural affinity
    + Trust
    + Experience
    ─────────────────
    = Psychic closeness
    ─────────────────

These relationships can also be represented by a model (see Fig. 2.3).

Cultural distance ████████████████████ Cultural affinity
        +   +
     Mistrust   ████████████████████   Trust
        +   +
  Social distance ████████████████████   Experience
        =   =
Psychic distance ████████████████████   Psychic Closeness

FIGURE 2.3

Therefore, when we come to describe and analyse relationships and interactions between UK and Japanese firms, it is important to grasp that psychic distance is being viewed as an amalgam of social distance, cultural distance and an element of trust/mistrust. It is worth making the point, too, that the concept of psychic distance has the added advantage of being able to be used in relation to the Interaction Approach that provides a well-established framework for investigating industrial buyer-seller relationships.

DISTANCE AND JAPAN

As Chapter 1 made clear, it is commonplace, when talking of business interactions with Japan, to find references and allusions to misunderstandings, communication gaps, language problems, and the like in all manner of dealings with Japanese organizations. These references and allusions were presented in a more or less general manner, but the various concepts of distance, and specifically the extended version of psychic distance described above, enable us to focus on the impact of these factors in more directed form.

In almost all business relationships and interactions involving Japanese and non-Japanese it appears to be generally recognized that intangible, yet sharply perceived elements, such as cross-cultural experience, personal and national affinities, trust, familiarity with other ways of doing business, knowledge of foreign languages and so forth, influence not only the business approach, but also the atmosphere of interactions and progression towards committed relationships.

This, however, is not the first time that the idea of applying distance factors to Japan has been mooted or applied. Holden (1991) has argued that 'it is impossible to study Japan, let alone do business with the Japanese anywhere on this planet, without being conscious of the heavy pall of psychic distance confusing mutual perceptions and interpretations of intentions'. A study by Holding (1988) examined psychic distance as a facet of interactions involving UK medical equipment manufacturers and customers in France, Germany, Italy, Japan, Sweden and the USA. This researcher established that psychic distance was most acutely felt in the interactions involving Japan, but experience of dealing with the Japanese market over time meant that 'business practices (were) less different from expected and trade barriers ... not as high as initially feared'. As far as the authors of this book are aware, the present study represents the first systematic attempt

JAPANESE-LED COMPANIES ●

to apply the concept of psychic distance to industrial interactions involving UK firms supplying technical goods to Japanese industrial customers. Also of note is our concern with Japanese industrial customers.

PART

2

Case studies of Anglo-Japanese interactions: the export relationships

Our policy shall be to evade any definite answer to their request, while at the same time maintaining a peaceful demeanour.

An adviser to the Shogun on how to deal with Western barbarians in 1854. Quoted in: Richard Storry, *A history of modern Japan* (1979).

Constant shilly-shallying, unbusinesslikeness almost passing belief.

Basil Hall Chamberlain, *Japanese Things* (1904/1982).

This chapter contains five case studies prepared by Abrahamsen. Each one describes the evolution of the relationship between a UK supplier of technical goods and its principal Japanese customer. The interactions are depicted with reference to one particular product line per informant company, and special attention is paid to those factors which create psychic distance.

METHODOLOGY

The five case studies presented below are a selection of ten prepared by Abrahamsen. They represent the fruits of a pilot study about firms' interactions with Japan and a follow-up study that attempted to investigate the impact of cultural factors and other influences which contribute to psychic distance. In the first phase information was gathered by using a standard IMP Group questionnaire that asks some 400 questions about several aspects of firms' involvements with foreign customers.

Using Japan as the market in question, the original ten informant companies provided extensive information on the following main topics: 1) the company background; 2) the development of focal relationships; 3) the characteristics of the exchange; 4) the organizational setting; 5) the relationship atmosphere and 6) connected relationships (i.e., the supplier and customer firms' business networks in the target market).

The questionnaire was used in face-to-face interviews. In all cases the company had been involved with supplying technical goods to the Japanese market for at least five years. The company respondent was invariably a senior manager with considerable experience of the particular Japanese customer and with extensive knowledge of the company, its policy and strategy. Respondents were invariably senior executives, sometimes chairmen and managing directors.

Having analysed data gathered from the ten informant companies, Abrahamsen proceeded to conduct face-to-face interviews with five of this original sample (see Table 3.1). An open-ended questionnaire was employed with the questions focusing on the impact of cultural issues on the investigated relationships (the term 'psychic distance' was not used with informants).

All companies investigated directed their marketing strategy towards particular niches in the Japanese market. The companies were all supplying industrial components, and products themselves were manufactured by highly specialized production techniques, often not available in Japan. Hence, the goods were generally low-volume and high capital-intensive. The companies in the sample were operating in markets with strong Japanese competition and their exporters' only competitive edge was their superior quality and product technology.

TABLE 3.1   The informant companies

NAME	PRODUCT	USE
Paper Industry Technologies Ltd.	Anti-deflection rolls	Paper
British Audio Systems Ltd.	Sound mixing consoles Music industry	Broadcasting
Delta (UK) Plc	Plastic masterbatches, pigmentation, protection	Pigmentation
Kamen Engineering Ltd.	Electrical switchgears	Metrosystems
AngloChem Plc	Industrial hardeners	Various

FORMAT OF THE CASE STUDIES

The case studies comprise four parts. Part A describes the background to the investigated relationship: in effect this is a summary of information from the pilot study. Part B distils the findings of the follow-up study. Part C analyses the impact of culture-related influences on relationship development and highlights factors that appear to create, and reduce, psychic distance. Part D highlights key learning points, based on the case study, for managing relationships with Japanese customers. A more general review of the findings, with some general management implications, is given in Chapter 4.

They just want our technology
Paper Industry Technologies Ltd.

The adoption and use of Western mechanical devices never presented any serious difficulties to peoples skilled in handicrafts that require nimble fingers and quick minds.
Sir George Sansom, *The Western World and Japan* (1950).

PART A   BACKGROUND TO THE RELATIONSHIP

Company background

Paper Industry Technologies Ltd. (PIT) produces capital-intensive heavy equipment for use in the paper industry. The product of particular interest in this case is anti-deflection rolls (drum-like devices which keep the supporting fabric of the paper level without implementing vibrations, thus keeping the width of the paper constant). Recently acquired by a medium-sized multinational corporation, its turnover in 1989 was £20m. In the UK it serves 25 customers, which represents a 90 per cent share of the market.

PIT, a Leeds-based operation, is heavily engaged in international activities with 80 per cent of its production output going to 100 customers worldwide. It has manufacturing subsidiaries in two overseas markets which account for five per cent of PIT's total production. There are plans to increase the number of these overseas production facilities over the next few years. Across its entire product range PIT faces 13 major international competitors, but as far as anti-deflection rolls are concerned, PIT is one of only five suppliers and claims to have a 50 per cent share of the market. The company is expecting a marked intensity of competitor activity over the next five years.

PIT has only one customer in Japan, the Yamagushi Corporation, who also acts as an intermediary supplying the UK firm's products on the Japanese market. All PIT's links with the Japanese market are channelled through Yamagushi. PIT estimates that the Yamagushi Corporation has about a 15 per cent share of the Japanese market. So far there is only one Japanese firm supplying anti-deflection rolls, but PIT and Yamagushi expect some rivals to enter the market over the coming years. Currently, PIT supply the Japanese firm's total requirement for anti-deflection rolls.

Development of the focal relationship

The relationship between PIT and the Yamagushi Corporation was initiated in 1985 (when the UK firm visited Japan on a trade mission), and the first delivery of anti-deflection rolls was made in 1986. Because of Yamagushi's strong position in the Japanese market, PIT was keen to become a business partner before a competitor stole a march on them. Otherwise the UK firm might have had very little chance of entering the Japanese market. In fact, gaining *any* foothold in the Japanese market was the dominant consideration at the time.

Since 1986 the sales pattern has been relatively stable. In 1990 sales were worth £170 000. Although the level of business is low, it is highly profitable and some increase is expected over the coming years.

Characteristics of the exchange

The anti-deflection rolls supplied by PIT do not differ dramatically from competitors' offerings, but in recent years the company has improved its production technology and so the firm considers that marginally it maintains technological leadership. Yamagushi likes to be associated with what it regards as innovative products. That the UK supplier is also outwardly keen to involve Yamagushi in joint specification is considered to have a positive motivating effect on the Japanese partner.

This involvement means that PIT consciously uses Yamagushi as a partner in technical development and also as a source of production ideas. The technical closeness is facilitated through 1) PIT's willingness to make product adaptations, and 2) Yamagushi's openness about sharing information both on technical issues and the state of the market, including the activities of competitors. The UK firm has even made modifications to its production processes to satisfy Yamagushi. However, there is a major problem.

Lurking in the mind of PIT is the fear that one day Yamagushi will have assimilated enough technological expertise to manufacture and market directly competing products. In fact, the UK chairman thinks that it was Yamagushi's interest in his firm's technology that initially sparked their enthusiasm to act as the intermediary for the Japanese market. As will become clear, this growing mistrust of Yamagushi's motives has been slowly undermining the quality of the relationship. There have also been clashes, described as 'frequent', that may be symbolic of the mutual wariness.

In the meantime, Yamagushi serves PIT as a bridgehead for business expansion into Japan, and the fact that PIT supplies the Japanese market, a notoriously difficult market, enhances its international image. But, in strict commercial terms, if PIT were to lose Yamagushi as a customer, it would only have a minor impact, whereas the consequences for the customer would be greater. In other words, Yamagushi's is more dependent on PIT than vice versa. It is, moreover, the view of PIT's chairman that it is his company, rather than the Japanese partner, who gains the greater overall benefit from the relationship.

Organizational setting

Despite the relatively small volume of business that PIT secures from Japan via Yamagushi, the relationship involves several personnel on both sides. Some seven PIT staff, from the chairman downwards, have contributed to the interactions; Yamagushi have 12 personnel involved. A good deal of the contact takes place at quite a senior level on both sides, covering the general commercial as well as technical aspects of the relationship. For example, PIT's additional services to the Yamagushi Corporation in the form of technical advice, and personnel training and instruction.

Direct day-to-day communication between PIT and Yamagushi, often on a fairly intensive basis, is mainly by telephone and fax; but there are two main face-to-face meetings each year, taking place in Japan and the UK. Yamagushi is, however, represented in London by one of the major Japanese trading companies. The junior manager with responsibility for Yamagushi is regarded by PIT as 'a foot soldier'. This individual, although he attends some of the UK meetings, has no influence over the PIT-Yamagushi relationship, but the chairman of the UK firm makes a point of meeting him on occasional visits to London and keeping him on the Christmas card list. To give a visible sign of commitment to the Japanese market, PIT have taken part in trade missions and a paper industry exhibition in Japan.

Relationship atmosphere

Despite PIT's preparedness to make product adaptations, despite some degree of openness about technical and commercial information on both sides, and despite the fact that good interpersonal relationships exist between representatives of the two firms, the atmosphere is not a good one. The UK firm's chairman is a visible and active participant in interactions, but almost certainly Yamagushi detect that neither he nor anyone else from PIT is really committed to the relationship.

PART B BUSINESS RELATIONSHIPS WITH JAPAN: PERCEPTIONS AND EXPERIENCES

The chairman of Paper Industry Technologies Ltd. said that the Japanese never really say what they mean. It was a nightmare to really understand their intentions. In his words:

> They take a whole day to say what they want, or rather what you think they want. They ply you with questions, and you do your best to answer them. But just when you think that you have understood the point of all their questions, they ask totally new questions. In the end you realise and you find that they are moving their position just to double-check everything.

This Japanese-style penchant for shifting the ground tended, from PIT's point of view, to make negotiations unnecessarily protracted, and this was a major source of irritation to the UK firm. Much of this 'ground-shifting' was most pronounced concerning technical matters. It was PIT's experience that, as soon as it had provided a solution to technical problems raised by Yamagushi, the Japanese partner 'would constantly bring up new problems'. All this suggested to PIT that Yamagushi were only interested in getting their hands on the UK firm's technology.

PIT, in effect, takes the view that it can only be a matter of time before Yamagushi introduce a directly competitive line. This conviction conditions all their interactions with the Japanese partner, and for this reason PIT is not prepared to make significant investments in the Japanese market. The company finds its business relationships with customers in South Korea and Taiwan more straightforward, certainly more lucrative, and there are no worries about the acquisition of technological expertise being central to those customers' business motivations. Countries like South Korea and Taiwan, said the chairman, 'may try to fool you, to manipulate you, they take bribes and all that, but they are really interested in doing business with you. That is not the case in Japan'. Not to put too fine a point on it: 'Yamagushi don't really want a genuine two-way involvement with us; they just want our technology'.

What the chairman grudgingly had to admire was 'the extreme patience' of the Japanese and their very polite persistence. He knew that Yamagushi would 'keep working with us, for years if necessary, to get what they want'. He felt that this politeness was a surface manifestation, and that the Japanese tendency to be polite actually inhibited rather than promoted friendly business relationships.

Politeness, though, was the Japanese way, and you could make allowance for it. But Yamagushi had a 'special practice', which has set the relationship on a downward path. As soon as the PIT engineers had established a good personal relationship with counterparts in Yamagushi, the Japanese company would move these personnel to other departments. In this way, the chairman claimed, Yamagushi could maintain a certain distance from the UK firm. It was hard to reconcile this with the much-vaunted emphasis in Japan on personal relationships. But it was what PIT regarded as the negative aspects of the interactions that forced the chairman to admit that the relationship had 'simply died away'.

The PIT chairman found the Japanese 'xenophobic'. They did not welcome foreign products. (He even claimed that 'foreigners are not welcome on the streets of Tokyo'.) Even though several trade barriers had been removed in recent years, cultural barriers still remained. He saw the hand of MITI promoting these non-tariff barriers as actively as it had promoted the formal ones in the past. 'Japanese industry prefers trading with Japanese companies', the chairman claimed. 'It's a closed shop – an old boy's club. It's difficult to get behind the front office.' It was a particularly hard club to join if you supplied industrial goods. The PIT chairman put it like this: 'All the stories about foreign successes in Japan are mostly Western companies selling up-market consumer goods like Scotch whisky and Gucci watches. For industrial manufacturers, it is a different story'.

To support his argument, the chairman referred to a case known to him personally where a Japanese producer was selling raw materials to Japanese manufacturers of paper rolls at lower prices than those offered by European manufacturers. PIT asked this company for a quotation, thinking it might secure some raw materials at low cost, only to discover that the Japanese company's price to them was double the price on the European market. In effect, the Japanese producer was conducting price discrimination between Japanese and foreign customers. 'This kind of protectionism is a part of the Japanese mentality', claimed the PIT chairman, adding, 'Japan is so out of balance with the rest of the world'. Nor were his impressions of Japanese protectionism of the paper industry market purely personal ones. Over the years he had spoken to various suppliers of equipment and products for use in the paper industry. Those with experience of doing business in Japan had all come to the same conclusion: the Japanese market was virtually closed to foreign companies.

On the basis of the commentary so far it might be thought that PIT, as personified by its chairman, were obtuse and did not take trouble to do homework on Japan. Yet representatives of PIT had attended conferences and seminars on how to do business in Japan. The chairman had read various publications produced by the British Government's Exports to Japan Unit, and also books on Japanese history and culture. He had shown a keen interest in Japanese business dealings: he presents his business card with a certain ritual solemnity; he expresses admiration for Japan; he astounds his Japanese hosts by eating raw fish. But neither he nor any other member of the company has attended a Japanese language course; the perception in the company is that Yamagushi personnel all have a sufficient knowledge of English for everyday business purposes. The chairman's view is that, even if his firm did have somebody able to speak and understand Japanese, this by itself would not transform communications, much less reduce the sense of wariness and disappointment that has crept into the relationship.

PART C FACTORS INFLUENCING THE IMPACT OF PSYCHIC DISTANCE

Although the PIT-Yamagushi relationship started very positively on both sides and still involves quite a large number of personnel in each company, the UK firm has found it difficult to understand the business objectives of the Japanese partner. Rightly or wrongly, PIT has come to the conclusion that the Japanese firm does not really want a 'normal' business relationship, but access to much-needed technological know-how. Despite this, PIT is still prepared to make investments in this relationship, no doubt partly because the direct marketing costs are not that heavy and Yamagushi is a stable purchaser.

At the personal level of interaction, language and communication problems have never been seen by PIT as a major issue. On the other hand, Yamagushi's constant probing for technical information has made PIT increasingly mistrustful of the Japanese firm's motives. Yamagushi's tendency to divert technical staff from the relationship adds sharply to the mistrust. All this in turn sets the scene for a reinforcement of the company's conviction that Japanese firms do business with non-Japanese firms under sufferance and to get access to their technological know-how. In this relationship the vicious circle is closed.

PART D   KEY LEARNING POINTS FOR MANAGING RELATIONSHIPS WITH JAPANESE CUSTOMERS

The PIT relationship atmosphere is characterized by a deep sense of *mistrust* of the Japanese partner. A whole gamut of factors conspired to create this atmosphere, according to PIT:

- problem of understanding Japanese business intentions
- Japanese penchant for 'ground-shifting'
- assumed Japanese interest in technology and not in a good business relationship
- MITI as the arch-villain
- uncertainties in handling and interpreting Japanese politeness
- Japanese xenophobia and protectionism
- price-rigging on the Japanese market
- prevalence of a view in the paper industry that Japanese firms are not to be trusted.

Important learning points:

- one prejudice about the Japanese and how to do business with them can be compounded with others
- *it is* difficult to understand Japanese business intentions; the Japanese do not always help themselves (nor their international image) in this respect.

Their ludicrous customs
British Audio Systems Ltd.

How utterly unreliable these people are if you take your eyes off them for a moment.
The Japan Diaries of Richard Gordon Smith (1858–1918), edited by V. Manthorpe (1986).

PART A   BACKGROUND TO THE RELATIONSHIP

Company background

British Audio Systems (BAS) Ltd. is an autonomous company with two individuals as major shareholders. The company, which is based in Manchester, has three separate business units: a broadcast division which manufactures sound mixing consoles for broadcasting; a music recording division which produces similar consoles for music recordings; and a sound reinforcement division. This case study will concentrate on the business relationships of the broadcasting division. The company's turnover in 1989 was £18m and this figure is expected to rise throughout the 1990s.

BAS enjoys a 25 per cent market share of the domestic market for its broadcasting products: eight competitors share the remaining 75 per cent. Nearly three-quarters of its entire output of these products is exported. On the Japanese market the presence of eight further competitors makes the competition stiffer, and the division manager (our main informant) estimates that BAS has an eight per cent share of the Japanese market.

BAS's powerful international position and its apparent success in the international arena must be seen in relation to its marketing strategy, which emphasizes niche marketing. In addition, the company has a clear understanding of consumers' preferences, as staff in key positions have prior experience from consumer-related activities and know their industry from the inside. It has also made a policy of building up relationships with exclusive distributors around the world, and has established a sales subsidiary in the United States (such arrangements are expected to increase in the future). In the Japanese market, there is a sole distributor who serves two roles. First, it purchases products from BAS as components for larger broadcasting consoles; second, it acts as an intermediary between BAS and their customers in the Japanese market.

Development of the focal relationship

The focal relationship between BAS and its intermediary, Kurosawa Broadcasting Inc., has existed since 1985. Annual sales have shown an upward trend and in 1989 Kurosawa purchased nearly half a million pounds worth of BAS equipment, involving 50 – 60 deliveries a year. Although the overall pattern of sales has been volatile and somewhat irregular, BAS expects to increase markedly the volume of its sales in Japan over the next five years.

Characteristics of the exchange

The technical quality and sophistication of BAS mixing consoles is a key ingredient in the product aspect of the relationship with Kurosawa. BAS quality is linked to their innovative production methods. Although BAS is strong enough to press its own technical standards on Kurosawa, it prefers to develop joint specification arrangements with the Japanese partner. This has enabled BAS equipment to become fully integrated with Kurosawa production requirements, while promoting an increasingly important technological partnership between the two firms. BAS's flexibility has certainly ensured that they supply 100 per cent of Kurosawa's need for mixing consoles, and that they can exploit the relationship for further penetration of the Japanese market. The fact that BAS supply Kurosawa carries weight in the Japanese sound and broadcasting industry.

BAS detects that Kurosawa perceives it to be a very important supplier and source of product ideas, as well as a potential catalyst for Kurosawa to export its complete sound systems to the UK market. On balance, BAS thinks that Kurosawa is more dependent on it than vice versa, and has

secured this position without making any major price or product concessions to the Japanese firm.

In order to facilitate business exchange to their mutual advantage, both
BAS and Kurosawa have made considerable adaptations. For example, the
Japanese customer has made changes in the specifications of their end
products, their stockholding policies and their payment procedures. Some
alterations have also been made in relation to production schedules and
processes. Less adaptations have been made by BAS, which bears out their
relative dominance in the relationship. But the UK firm has made significant changes for its Japanese customer in 'non-production areas' such as
maintenance, service, provision of technical updates and other business
information. Interestingly, BAS has introduced quality control procedures
under Kurosawa's influence. However, as we shall discover presently, the
UK firm does not regard the cooperation as a particularly notable aspect
of the relationship.

Organizational setting

The relationship is handled by three BAS personnel and seven members
of staff at Kurosawa. One of the Kurosawa staff is designated as the permanent link person for BAS. Three main joint meetings to review performance
and future strategy are held every year, normally in Tokyo. In between times
there is steady contact between Manchester and Tokyo by fax and telephone, perhaps 150 such contacts each year.

Relationship atmosphere

To a large extent the atmosphere surrounding the BAS-Kurosawa relationship is determined by the more or less dominant position of the UK firm.
Kurosawa's dependence on BAS is enhanced since both firms know that
BAS has alternatives to the relationship, in the Japanese market. Thus BAS
has never had to make major − that is, unduly onerous − concessions
to the Japanese customer. This also explains why the relative intensity of
everyday business interactions does not involve active forms of cooperation, concerning joint technical development, for example.

BAS's division manager for broadcasting products said that the level of cooperation was 'rather low'. He is aware that the 'logic' of the relationship is such that much closer technical interaction should be taking place, but he has little confidence in the information provided by Kurosawa Broadcasting Inc. Not only that: he feels that their Japanese customer withholds important information and is prepared to exploit the relationship for their own advantage. Thus a certain mistrust, which may well be mutual, has begun to cast a shadow over the relationship.

The same BAS manager was conscious of a general communication gap between his company and Kurosawa. He thought that much of the problem was due to language difficulties which, in his experience, were not alleviated, but rather added to, by interpreters (BAS always hire one) and the Kurosawa personnel 'who think they can speak English'.

Part B BUSINESS RELATIONSHIPS WITH JAPAN: PERCEPTIONS AND EXPERIENCES

The division manager argued that absolutely every aspect of his interactions with his Japanese customer, Kurosawa Broadcasting Co., was constrained by the language barrier. It was his practice to hire an interpreter – invariably female – from an agency. Not only was this 'somewhat costly', but, more crucially, he had the nagging fear that the interpreters failed to understand, and therefore convey to Kurosawa, what he called his 'concepts' – his ideas and intentions about the business at hand. No wonder he had to keep going to Japan. Sooner or later the Japanese would understand and then some of them might actually bother to take up his repeated invitations to visit BAS headquarters in Manchester.

But there was another problem connected with information exchange. Kurosawa, it seemed to him, was simply not interested in giving him 'nonsecret' business information. This was a constant source of personal irritation, as he felt that exchanging information about customers and markets was perfectly normal practice. Thus he came to view the Japanese as secretive. In order to stimulate the flow of information, he resorted to the tactic

of 'being non-Japanese', by which he meant being outlandish and consciously infringing the 'don'ts' of the general principles of how to do business with the Japanese. This tactic was all the more baffling because the
UK manager claimed to have made a careful study of the Japanese business style. One ploy was to be 'persistent and demanding'; another was
to do 'something unusual'.

The manager related how he once asked the office ladies out for lunch
when visiting the head office of Kurosawa Broadcasting Inc. This episode
was viewed with dismay and confusion by the Japanese executives (as anyone familiar with Japan can imagine). Unabashed, the BAS manager took
great pride at having acted against the normal conventions, stating that
'being plain-speaking Northerners, we tell them what we mean and don't
take formalities seriously'. He justified his action on the grounds that the
Japanese do not approve of foreigners who slavishly follow Japanese practices such as deep bowing, exaggerated presentations of business cards,
indulging in long pauses and so forth (and there is some truth in this conviction). Therefore, a foreigner could, after all, be a foreigner, and he even
considered that he had 'educated' many Japanese through his particular
style of not being Japanese!

In everyday business dealings, he found the Japanese to be 'passively
defensive, but non-aggressive'. He wished though that Kurosawa would give
more decision-making authority to the middle managers with whom he had
to deal: that would make his job much more straightforward and reduce
the inordinate amount of time spent in negotiations. It was his hunch that,
if he could strike up good personal relationships, it would somehow put
an end to the endless discussions over the same old small points. He could
then avoid 'all those large discussions'.

As it happened, he had struck up some good personal relationships
with Kurosawa staff, but it was a source of disappointment to him that none
of them had ever invited him to their home. He could not reconcile this
with the big emphasis in Japan on lavish business entertainment. But what
irritated him most was the habitual Japanese reluctance to admit failure,
even when the failure was clearly theirs. Worse, they would put up a 'ludicrous explanation that has no validity'. This he attributed to the Japanese

fear of losing face.

The BAS manager could never quite get over 'their ludicrous customs'. One of these was gift-giving, and, connected with that, the strange habit of wrapping everything up. In fact, in Japan, he said 'they actually pay more attention to the wrapping rather than content. It's absolutely ludicrous' (everything about Japan was 'ludicrous'). He was equally dismissive of Japanese music, admittedly an acquired taste — somewhat ironic for someone supplying sound equipment.

Part c FACTORS INFLUENCING THE IMPACT OF PSYCHIC DISTANCE

The most important factor binding BAS and Kurosawa is the excellence of the UK audio mixing consoles and the Japanese firm's clear intention to remain the exclusive purchaser. This has certainly made the relationship become profitable for BAS, but the likelihood of major joint business development appears mainly to be handicapped by the tactless, occasionally oafish, behaviour of the BAS manager responsible for the Japanese market.

Although he is surely right to stress the problem of the language barrier; although he may feel, with some justification, that Kurosawa is unnecessarily secretive; although he may think that Japanese culture gets in the way of getting down to business: the fact remains that this particular individual almost certainly conveys to his Japanese counterparts an image of peculiar quaintness (which can just about be tolerated) and of disagreeable forthrightness (which is less easily tolerated).

His deliberate 'flaunting' of many unwritten rules of interactions between Japanese and foreigners (see Chapter 4) may, if he is lucky, strike his hosts as typical of foreigners who cannot be expected to know better. If, beyond that, the UK manager displays what the Japanese would interpret as disdain for Japanese culture, this means that the relationship is proceeding under sufferance. No wonder that his Japanese partners appear reluctant to visit BAS in the UK.

To conclude: here is the case of an individual who prides himself on having studied the 'dos and don'ts' of dealing with the Japanese in business, and can still manage not to notice how variously comic and offensive his behaviour is to his counterparts. Moreover, his company appears not to notice that he is the wrong man to be dealing with the Japanese, and may even be a major constraint on future business development.

PART D KEY LEARNING POINTS FOR MANAGING RELATIONSHIPS WITH JAPANESE CUSTOMERS

This relationship is, in a sense, dominated by a UK export representative whom the Japanese customer almost certainly finds odd and even, on occasions, insufferable (no wonder Kurosawa do not appear willing to accept invitations to visit the BAS base in the UK). Here the indifferent quality of the relationship, to a large degree, can be put down to the fact that the BAS representative has no sense of being an intruder in Japanese society. He is an example of the *wrong kind of person for dealing with Japanese customers*. He creates problems in the relationships by:

- making no modification to his personal behaviour
- failing to note that he, as much as the Japanese, is responsible for language problems
- deriding the Japanese way of doing business
- finding everything Japanese 'ludicrous'
- failing to realize that the Japanese reluctance to pass on business information may well be a personal snub.

Important learning points:

- The person who comes over as an oaf in Japan will almost certainly be oafish at home too. Sometimes oafs are heavily disguised as worldly-wise 'good blokes' (*un*internationally-minded personnel departments, please note), but their capacity to handle business relationships in Japan is severely limited.
- The oaf is seldom able to understand how to modify his spoken English to make himself more intelligible and personally attractive to the Japanese.

- Deriding local culture is the hallmark of ignorance; what faith can the firm back home put in such a person's judgements about other peoples and their way of doing business?
- The oaf is someone who would not see any point in reading this book!

I'm a businessman, not an anthropologist

Delta (UK) Plc

The princes were always friendly, conversable, and unwearied questioners respecting European arts, sciences, customs, and manners ... but they never alluded to Japanese policy.

Philipp Franz von Siebold, *Manners and Customs of the Japanese* (1841).

PART A   BACKGROUND TO THE RELATIONSHIP

Company background

Delta (UK) Plc is a major subsidiary of a large US multinational with global interests in the chemical, biochemical and food-processing industries. For its part, Delta specializes in manufacturing and marketing raw materials, notably masterbatches, for the plastics industry on a worldwide basis. In this case study the products of interest are processed masterbatches and components for pigmentation and ultra-violet protection.

Seventy per cent of Delta's output is produced in five countries outside the UK, although the UK represents 35 per cent of its total worldwide sales. The company has sales subsidiaries in over 90 countries. The managing director, the main informant for this case study, estimates the company's worldwide market share to be around five per cent, and expects all of their international activities to increase over the coming years.

Although Delta is a major player, the entire industry – even for masterbatches – is made up of an indefinite number of suppliers. The market is characterized by a situation where customers and competitors often are one and the same. Delta estimate that, as far as masterbatches are concerned, they have in excess of a thousand customers worldwide. In this case study the selected customer is Kashimawa Inc., a member of one of Japan's largest diverse corporations. Kashimawa accounts for 12 per cent of Delta's sales in the Japanese market, the UK firm catering for 25 per cent of the customer's need for processed masterbatches and components.

Development of the focal relationship

Delta's relationship with Kashimawa Inc. dates back to 1964. For many years business was stable, but in the last five years there has been a rapid increase in sales, and in 1989 Delta supplied some 12 000 tons of processed masterbatches and components. On present trends, the UK firm expects modest increases in volumes sold over the next five years.

Characteristics of the exchange

Although Delta does not use production technology that is in any way revolutionary for manufacturing masterbatches for the plastics industry, the process is a tricky one. As a result Delta has managed to supply consistently high-quality products, and, given the industry it is in, it is the manufacturers not customers who fix specifications – customers buy available grades. This situation applies equally to Kashimawa, but over the years Delta has made efforts to develop specific grades for this Japanese customer for whom plastics masterbatches play an important role in their production processes. Delta is continually aware that underperformance of its masterbatches can have very serious consequences for Kashimawa and its customers in Japan. The fact that Delta has consistently met this customer's requirements for over 25 years means that the business relationship is close to being institutionalized.

Delta makes about 10 deliveries a year to Kashimawa. It is profitable business for Delta, and the managing director has reason to believe that Kashimawa benefits from the security of having a long-term, dependable supplier who is non-Japanese. 'This helps to keep other Japanese suppliers on their toes', was Delta's argument.

Organizational setting

Direct interactions take place three times a year in Tokyo. The main business talking point concerns the scale and scheduling of future deliveries. Otherwise contact is maintained by fax and telephone, these exchanges occurring every two to three weeks. This relatively intermittent pattern of contact is consistent with a relationship which is based on sales and some limited technical exchanges. Five Delta personnel have various degrees of direct responsibility for progressing business with Kashimawa. For its part, the Japanese firm fields ten members of staff to liaise with Delta.

Relationship atmosphere

Kashimawa is only one of twenty customers served by Delta in Japan, but is one of its more important ones, accounting for 12 per cent of its total sales in that market. Delta's view is that Kashimawa is more dependent on Delta than vice versa. Although there is a certain amount of technical exchange between the two firms, the relationship is marked by the low degree of cooperation. It is very much a sales relationship and Delta's perception of Kashimawa is that the Japanese customer is not interested in things being otherwise. Kashimawa is always pressing for lower prices and discounts, and is ever quick to seek compensation in the event of (alleged) sea-damage to the product.

There is, in fact, not much trust between the two companies, and Kashimawa reveals very little about its own customers. This reluctance on the part of Kashimawa to open up the relationship has laid the ground for misunderstandings and mistrust. Language problems do not come into it: 'it's more fundamental'. The managing director feels that he receives little attention from Kashimawa Inc. Kashimawa did not understand, and did not care about their problems as a supplier. As will be noted below, these feelings have led from time to time to antagonisms, even sharp clashes, in the relationship. Despite this, the two companies have learned to tolerate each other, and Delta have to admit that Kashimawa has been a fundamentally loyal customer.

PART B BUSINESS RELATIONSHIPS WITH JAPAN: PERCEPTIONS AND EXPERIENCES

Delta's managing director admitted that he found it very difficult to fathom out the Japanese approach to business and to handle interpersonal exchanges, especially when questions, that were bound to put the Japanese on the spot, elicited evasive responses. On such occasions, he noted, 'the Japanese would just be looking at us instead of answering the question, and we would not know what was going through their minds'. Similarly: 'during negotiations, the Japanese have a practice of not answering freely, merely gazing at you without saying anything when I face them with a difficult question'.

The managing director found these episodes 'very tedious', all the more so as, on his own admission, he had never bothered to really understand the Japanese and what motivated them. In fact he found the incessant emphasis on culture irksome. 'I'm a businessman, not an anthropologist!', he protested. He could not understand all the ritual associated with exchanges of business cards − and all those albums they have, chock-a-block with business cards picked up years ago! And why, now that Delta knew its Japanese customers so well (and there were some good relationships at the personal level), did the business discussions have to proceed on such formal lines? It was a mystery to him why one of his colleagues, Roy Berry, who had been dealing with Kashimawa for 27 years, was still called 'Berry-san' by the Kashimawa manager who had taken him to his home at least twenty times in as many years.

As for the Japanese as business partners (not just Kashimawa), he found them to be highly efficient, very hard-working, extremely dedicated and determined. He also noted a feeling of inferiority (was it really inferiority?) and a 'low degree of self-confidence'. But the factor which made the deepest impression on him was the fact that the Japanese 'always seem to know everything about you before you even have met them, and seem to know what you want long before you have started negotiating with them'.

He also noted a Japanese tendency to 'try out' new business partners by putting all kinds of demands on them when entering a new business relationship. It had been his experience that 'the Japanese will not do business with you if you don't pass the test and if they think you are incompetent'. If you gave in, they would always take advantage of you. The only way to avoid this, he claimed, was to be 'strong and not let the Japanese have their way'.

He had noted too that the Japanese got 'very upset' if Delta failed to provide technical information or if the company delivered, even slightly, behind schedule. Broken promises, in Japanese eyes, were serious infringements of trust. The fact that they might beat Delta down on price for late delivery or container damage, but resell the affected Delta product to their domestic customers at the originally agreed price – well, that was different.

PART C   FACTORS INFLUENCING THE IMPACT OF PSYCHIC DISTANCE

Delta's managing director needed no reminding that the Japanese were different. Acknowledging this, he did some homework on Japan: he read the odd article and had even sought the advice of the British government's Exports to Japan Unit ('But what do they know?', he grimaced). But he wanted to treat the Japanese as normal businessmen; he found it difficult, almost irksome, to regard them as a sort of special case. He thought that he had done his bit to establish a good working relationship. But the Japanese side were not prepared to open up: they were not forthcoming about information; business discussions would drag on over trivia; they were non-committal about new proposals and ideas; they were not interested in Delta's problems as a supplier – so, when Delta did not quite meet delivery schedules, there was only implied criticism. Kashimawa was a loyal customer, but it was not to be trusted.

Although Delta's managing director was aware that there was some kind of explanation for the Japanese behaviour, he was not particularly interested to find out what it was. From his own account we can surmise that he was probably never entirely able to conceal or disguise his irritated mystification at the Japanese way of doing things; that he perhaps came across as a very impatient business partner; and that he appeared to lack finesse in his interpersonal relationships.

As managing director of his company, and therefore the most authoritative symbol of its commitment and capability, his behaviour and attitudes counted for rather more in Japanese eyes than he perhaps appreciated. We may conclude that, at best, the two companies have learned to tolerate each other and, despite the ups and downs, to sustain a mutually advantageous relationship for more than a quarter of a century.

PART D KEY LEARNING POINTS FOR MANAGING RELATIONSHIPS WITH JAPANESE CUSTOMERS

This long-term relationship is characterized by growing mistrust and a lack of cooperation, despite some 25 years of business involvement between Delta and Kashimawa. However, major factors in the situation appear to be the Delta representative's difficulties in handling interpersonal exchanges and grasping the Japanese approach to business – despite some attempts to come to grips with Japanese business culture through background reading and discussions with some sources of authoritative knowledge. The root of the problem seems to be that the Delta representative could not reconcile himself to accept that, really, *you have to treat Japanese businesses in special ways*. For this reason he had developed a certain disparaging view of the Japanese, while denigrating their business customs. The Japanese had, according to him:

• an inferiority complex
• low self-esteem.

They were also likely to:
- withold important business information
- impose unnecessary demands to test the relationship
- drag out business discussions
- get 'very upset' if Delta failed, even slightly, to live up to a promise or keep a deadline.

Important learning points:
- Years of personal and corporate experience of doing business in Japan do not necessarily mean insight and expertise in handling relationships with Japan customers. In fact, the years of experience can reinforce firmly held prejudices.
- Learning about Japan can be confusing – even emotionally and intellectually painful.

Ordinary people with a different work ethic

Kamen Engineering Ltd.

The more formal a society, the more obvious the roles people play. In this respect the Japanese are quite scrutable.
Ian Buruma, *A Japanese Mirror* (1988)

PART A BACKGROUND TO THE RELATIONSHIP

Company background

Kamen Engineering Ltd., a subsidiary of a large British multinational company, is a leading manufacturer of electrical switchgears and other electrical plant for heavy industrial purposes. Its head office and principal works are in Newcastle. Business is conducted in terms of contract work, and the company has carried out different projects in various parts of the world. Eighty per cent of its total business comes from the UK market, with major contracts from manufacturers of North Sea oil rigs. Even so, Kamen likes to think of itself as a company with a strong international orientation.

Switchgear manufactured by Kamen Engineering Ltd. – the product of interest in this case study – is very specialized, and competition in this area is limited to eight producers worldwide. Three of these are Japanese. Despite this major source of competition, Kamen has succeeded in securing substantial orders from the Yashita Corporation of Nagoya, which operates worldwide as a main contractor for large scale industrial projects involving the installation of heavy electrical plants.

Development of the focal relationship

The relationship with Yashita dates back to 1986 when the Japanese firm approached Kamen for specialized equipment, of which they were one of five manufacturers worldwide. Business developed, but only after 'a long tedious process'. Kamen's most notable success was in supplying equipment to the Yashita Corporation who had been appointed as main contractor for the construction of an underground railway system for a South-East Asian government. This resulted in a £1m contract in 1989. Another major contract for a similar project is currently under negotiation.

If Kamen win this second major contract, it will boost current sales turnover by 40 per cent. Even if this contract should not materialize, Kamen's contracts manager, the informant for this case study, is optimistic that his company will continue to be a very important – and reliable – supplier to Yashita over years to come.

Characteristics of the exchange

Yashita is already very important to Kamen and has the potential to be the UK firm's biggest single customer. The fact that Kamen has succeeded, over five years, in building up to supplying an estimated 10 per cent of

Yashita's requirements for heavy electrical switchgear is a notable achievement, bearing in mind that, to some extent, Yashita has almost certainly been placing correspondingly less business with its traditional Japanese suppliers.

According to Kamen, its success has been in part due to its production technology which is considered superior to that employed by their Japanese competitors. Kamen, noting how keen Yashita is to be associated with innovative production technology, has made considerable efforts not only to involve the Japanese customer in joint specifications, but to try to understand their business mentality.

Organizational setting

Responsibility for day-to-day handling of the relationship is carried by two Kamen personnel and five members of staff from Yashita. One of the Kamen personnel is the contracts manager, who devotes a very high proportion of his work time to controlling the relationship. When a sizeable contract is under negotiation, there may be as many as 12 joint discussions in one month in Newcastle and Nagoya. At other times, the contracts manager makes two visits a year to Japan, to review the state of fulfilment of current contracts and to prospect for future business. Owing to the relatively fast build-up of business (after the slow start), Kamen have appointed a retired senior executive from one of the major trading houses to act as an intermediary. A high proportion of the communications pass through his hands. This arrangement appears to be working satisfactorily: it ensures that Yashita gets continuity of attention and that Kamen is promptly alerted to any change in requirements.

Relationship atmosphere

Kamen's contracts manager described the relationship with Yashita as 'very healthy'. In the beginning Kamen had made several product adaptations and granted some concessions on price to secure the first set of contracts. This flexibility led directly to the £1m contract in 1989. Although Kamen's dependence on Yashita is greater than vice versa, the Japanese company is very dependent on Kamen's technological expertise and high product performance, which have become part of the package purchased by their customer. As the contracts manager tellingly put it: 'once the contract is signed, you're in the driving seat'.

Although there is close consultation between the two firms, Kamen feels that Yashita is not always prepared to understand supplier problems. On the other hand, when there have been instances of late delivery, it has imposed a certain strain on the relationship because it normally means that Yashita has to reschedule deliveries to its customers, and this means loss of face. Despite such set-backs, a high degree of trust exists in the relationship — to the extent that Yashita are relatively open about their customers.

To create this atmosphere, the UK contracts manager has taken great pains skilfully to play down the importance of the legally-binding aspects of their interactions, in order to stress the 'gentleman's word is his bond' approach. He believes that this appeals to the Japanese psychology and helps draw the two companies together. All this, though, has entailed Kamen in an intense learning process about their Japanese partners. But perhaps the most characteristic aspect of the atmosphere is the way in which the UK contracts manager has, very astutely, personalized the relationship.

PART B BUSINESS RELATIONSHIPS WITH JAPAN: PERCEPTIONS AND EXPERIENCES

At the outset of the relationship the contracts manager found that he had to make several personal adjustments to Japanese culture, and social interactions with Yashita personnel in and outside the company environment. He used to be surprised by the large number of people who would arrive at meetings and then sit in silence. It was very difficult to determine either their status within the company or their actual relationship with the business involving Kamen and Yashita. Some of these people he described as 'dummies': their job was obviously to help create the kind of atmosphere desired by Yashita. But he has adjusted to the fact that 'one or two people will hold court, normally the most senior people, while the rest will just sit there patiently and listen'. He got used to the interminable discussions; but he knew that he was dealing with 'very good businessmen'. Language problems were frequently acute; so the vital thing was to learn to listen rather than keep pushing forward his own point of view.

He also learnt that there was no point in being 'uptight' about the Japanese penchant for secrecy and their tendency, even when inebriated, never to drop their formal guard completely. What counted with the Japanese, he realized, was not just commitment, but *display of commitment*. And display of commitment was primarily achieved through intense personalization of the relationship. He, the contracts manager, began to symbolize to Yashita the commitment and capabilities of Kamen. The degree of personalization of the relationship was articulated in this comment: 'there is only one person besides myself in our company that I would trust to deal with the Japanese. It is difficult, if not impossible, to deal with them if they suspect lack of commitment. ... The Japanese can spot non-committed people a mile off'.

Realizing that display of commitment through personalization of the relationship was central to relationship-building with his Japanese customer, the contracts manager discovered that he had resolved an important conundrum about dealing with the Japanese – at least, as far as his own experience was concerned. The Japanese, in their heart of hearts, could never fully trust non-Japanese business partners ('it's in their nature'), but they did respond to displays of commitment. For their part, Western firms found it hard to communicate with Japanese companies, and complained of Japanese deception and evasion. Once you accepted that these Japanese tendencies were rooted in a desire to avoid confrontation (and rash promises), learning to understand Japanese customers was far more straightforward.

Having reached this point in his thinking, he had no time for notions of the Japanese being 'mystical and unique'. As far as he was concerned, 'they are ordinary people but with a different work ethic'. Armed with this conviction and being prepared to get to know his business partners thoroughly ('endless social evenings'), the contracts manager found the Japanese to be 'very friendly and pleasant to do business with'. On his last trip to Japan (December 1990), he had discovered 'a refreshing openness'. In his words: 'It seemed like they had made a corporate decision to become committed to us. This is very promising for our further dealings with them, even though they have not yet formally given us the new contract. When we first tried to negotiate with them, we were just another company. Now we are a major business partner'.

It is worth noting that the contracts manager became extremely interested in Japan – he read about Japanese culture and history; he attended courses in the UK on doing business in Japan (one of which was organized by Yashita's London office); he took advice from people, including the staff of the Commercial Section of the British Embassy in Tokyo ('they were actually useful!'); and, not to be overlooked, he drew on nearly 20 years' experience of international negotiation of complex industrial contracts – so he was a man who knew how to bide his time, but also how to strike at the opportune moment. He estimates that from the first encounter with Kamen in 1986 it took two years of quite close involvement before he began to gain a clear grasp of the Japanese business psychology. This is, indeed, a very considerable achievement.

He had two overriding concerns about the Japanese: they worked too hard and they were too formal. On the first point he observed that 'the Japanese work more than is good for them, and their efficiency declines as a function of their workload'. Concerning the second point, he thought that dealing with Yashita would be much easier 'if the Japanese were more relaxed and less formal'.

PART C   FACTORS INFLUENCING THE IMPACT OF PSYCHIC DISTANCE

Kamen's experiences of the Japanese market replicate many of those which have been highlighted in the previous three case studies: language problems, mistrust, Japanese secretiveness, Japanese unwillingness to understand supplier problems, interminable discussions, and so forth. Yet the case of Kamen suggests how the almost natural tendency of Japanese and non-Japanese to miscommunicate, misunderstand and mistrust each other can be surmounted to evolve straightforward, harmonious business relationships.

However, while it might appear that Kamen is a shining example of doing things the right way, the proper evaluation is that the company is lucky enough to have a highly experienced contracts manager who has understood the business mentality of his Japanese business partners. On his own admission, and with a high degree of personal involvement with Yashita, it took him two years to gain this knowledge – and he was a man who was actively looking for it. (Compare him with the BAS manager in the previous case study.) But, bearing in mind the extent to which he has personalized the commitment and actively excluded all but one other colleague from close involvement with Yashita, the relationship has an exposed flank: it could be dangerously weakened if he were, for whatever reason, to cease working for Kamen.

PART D   KEY POINTS FOR MANAGING RELATIONSHIPS WITH JAPANESE CUSTOMERS

The vital aspect of this case study is that it shows the potentially large payoff which stems from gaining a *clear understanding of the Japanese business psychology*. This kind of understanding seems to come from a willingness to deal with the Japanese without negative prejudices and to treat them, from the beginning, as trusted partners. The Kamen experience represents a marked contrast to the first three case studies, and we should note the importance of additional factors such as:

- deployment of a strategy based on 'a gentleman's word is his bond' (which resonates very closely with the Japanese ideal of fulfilling promises and obligations);
- personalizing the relationships with the Japanese customers, which is only possible through 1) personal adaptations, 2) establishment of a trusting atmosphere, and 3) a demonstrated professional approach;
- a recognition of the complexity of language problems;

- not being too concerned that the Japanese side is not always supplying information.

Important learning points:

- the capacity to be patient and to pay close attention to all forms of Japanese behaviour
- the value of international experience — the development of a certain cross-cultural *savoir-faire*
- it may take two years of several short visits to understand the Japanese business psychology
- knowing how to speak English patiently and clearly with Japanese counterparts is one of the most valuable assets of the would-be negotiator.

Total involvement: the single most important factor to the Japanese customer *AngloChem Plc*

They have rites and customs so different from those of all other nations that it seems that they deliberately try to be unlike any other people. The things they do in this respect are beyond imagining and it may truly be said that Japan is a world the reverse of Europe.

Alessandro Valignano, S.J. (1539–1606). Quoted in:
Michael Cooper (ed.) *They came to Japan.*

PART A BACKGROUND TO THE RELATIONSHIP

Company background

AngloChem plc was founded at the turn of the century, manufacturing a wide range of chemicals for industrial and civil engineering applications:

hardeners for epoxy resins, coatings, adhesives and composites and civil engineering applications. In this case study the product line of interest is hardening compounds.

AngloChem is based in Wolverhampton, where it has its main UK production facility. But it has plants in two other countries, that account for 60 per cent of the company's total production. It has fully-fledged sales subsidiaries in four countries. Forty-five per cent of the Wolverhampton production is exported. Japan, where AngloChem serves 30 customers, is considered its most important export market. As an indication of its relative success on the Japanese market, AngloChem claims to have forced three local competitors out of business (a rare example of role-reversal).

Development of the focal relationship

AngloChem has been supplying the Japanese market since 1970. It sells directly to Nippon Trading Corporation (NTC), one of Japan's major trading groups, who distribute AngloChem's products to 30 end-users in Japan. This relationship was initiated by AngloChem Plc in a search for a suitable Japanese trading partner. AngloChem's technical director, the informant for this case study, stresses that its relatively strong position in the Japanese market has been due to the development of a healthy relationship with NTC, which exercises enormous economic power both inside and outside Japan.

As an indication of the current scale of business, a forty-ton AngloChem container is delivered every week to the port of Tokyo. In 1990, this meant sales to the value of £3.5m and represents the culmination of rapid increases by NTC over the last five years. All the signs are that the scale of business will increase throughout the 1990s.

Characteristics of the exchange

NTC buy from AngloChem a specific range of industrial hardeners, whose performance is closely specified by the NTC on behalf of their customers. The product for Japan represents a significant modification of the standard product and entails manufacturing difficulties for AngloChem. For example, AngloChem discovered that the Japanese have very sensitive noses, and one important modification concerned changing the smell of the product ('a very tricky process'). But the willingness of AngloChem to meet customer requirements so closely has been a major positive influence on the relationship with NTC, contributing to what both regard as a healthy and profitable business.

NTC is AngloChem's sole customer in Japan, and NTC is the sole supplier of industrial hardeners. However, AngloChem regards NTC as much more than an exclusive buyer of a range of its products. The strongly-developed relationship serves as an incentive for NTC to find new customers and new applications for AngloChem products in Japan. This brings with it a useful spin-off to AngloChem – the relationship with NTC is a valuable source of product ideas. The fact that AngloChem has had such long-standing success on the Japanese market, universally perceived as hard to enter and as having exceptionally high quality and performance requirements, adds to AngloChem's prestige and influence with customers in other countries.

Even more significantly, AngloChem Plc places great importance on a number of facets of its relationship with the Nippon Trading Corporation, such as the amount NTC buys from them and the range of products sold, a source of product ideas, a bridgehead for expansion in Japan and as an image enhancer. Likewise, AngloChem Plc sees itself as important to the Nippon Trading Corporation for largely the same reasons. It also takes the trouble to translate company brochures and technical literature into Japanese.

The importance the parties attach to each other is exemplified by the fact that a termination of the relationship would have serious effects for both of them. The technical director estimates that the profitability for both parties has been, and is, very good. Thus a high degree of interdependence has become established between AngloChem and NTC. The present position is that if NTC were to lose AngloChem as supplier, or if AngloChem lost NTC as a customer, the consequences would, according to the technical director, be 'very serious' for both companies.

Organizational setting

Over the years, AngloChem and NTC have established routines for deal-ing with each other, but the crucial factor, as far as intercompany relation-ships are concerned, is that NTC acts both as customer and intermediary. AngloChem never goes behind NTC's back to meet the end-users. Meet-ings with end-users, either in NTC's Tokyo head office or at the end-users' works, are always arranged and attended by NTC personnel.

AngloChem has 12 personnel involved with the business with NTC; for its part, the Japanese company involves 15 people in its chemicals divi-sion. Face-to-face meetings in Tokyo take place every two months; inter-mittent meetings take place between AngloChem and NTC at the latter's London office. At the meetings in Japan the technical director is invaria-bly impressed with the preparation undertaken by the Japanese partner: facts and figures are available on everything.

Apart from these meetings, which are concerned with monitoring the state of current orders and reviewing future business, there is quite heavy contact by telephone and fax between the two companies. The technical director, who devotes around 10 per cent of his time to the relationship with NTC, estimates that there is some long-distance contact every day of the year. Although many of the communications are to do with technical queries, normal sales enquiries, confirmations of orders, container schedul-ings and deliveries, this is considered an extremely important aspect of the relationship: the Japanese always like to know the status of order and en-quiries, and prompt handling is seen as a sign of commitment and efficiency.

Relationship atmosphere

The relationship atmosphere is marked by a strong degree of interdepen-dence, without one party or the other seeming to have the upper hand. There is a high degree of mutual trust. AngloChem does not believe that NTC is going to switch its suppliers for industrial hardeners; AngloChem is certainly not intending to exploit any other links it has in the Japanese market. As the technical director explains: 'Dealing with the Japanese is all a question of mutual trust. Trust takes a long time to build up, but once they know you, you're in'. The level of mutual trust, and the resulting mutual commitment and loyalty, took 20 years to develop.

For his part, the technical director has made efforts to study Japanese history, culture and business customs, and he believes that these efforts have helped greatly in reducing cultural differences and problems of mis-communication. Over the years, he has been a frequent guest at the home of his NTC counterparts, and practically no Japanese would make this gesture to a foreigner unless there was genuine regard. He has also spent many, many social evenings, eating and drinking with his NTC counterparts. All this, he feels, has brought him, and therefore AngloChem, much closer to NTC. But in addition to the personal aspect to atmosphere, the technical director was convinced that previous satisfactory experience with the product – everything from reliable performance to prompt delivery – all contributed actively to the relationship's quality.

PART B   BUSINESS RELATIONSHIPS WITH THE JAPANESE: PERCEPTIONS AND EXPERIENCES

According to the technical director, Japanese customers 'tend to be very loyal once you have developed a relationship'. But this is predicated on an ability to achieve high product quality standards, standards which are a good deal higher than for customers elsewhere. He added: 'once it is proved that you are capable of making high-quality products and that there is a sincere commitment to a long-term relationship, the Japanese will not question you'. On the other hand, they will be very quick to let you know if you fall short of their high standards. But you can redeem things some-what by sorting out mishaps fast (after apologizing profusely), especially if the result is an improvement in product performance.

The technical director is fairly certain that AngloChem has received far more complaints concerning product attributes from their Japanese cus-tomer than their European or American customers. In fact, he considered that meeting the Japanese quality standards was the most difficult factor in dealing with the Nippon Trading Corporation. Quality was not merely required in terms of product performance and reliability, it also related to delivery and service. What the Japanese wanted, he said, was 'total quality', which he described as a complex fusion of the technical, human and psychological aspects of the business relationship.

'Part of the game', as he put it, was to ensure that you satisfied, and did not question, the Japanese fetish for quality. He gave an example of what he meant: some years ago, NTC had asked if a particular chemical compound manufactured by AngloChem would meet the performance requirements laid down by the end-users. It was not good enough for Anglo-Chem to state that this compound only partially met requirements and to suggest that they could modify it accordingly; NTC still insisted on obtaining the specification of this component. It was not that NTC did not believe AngloChem. The technical director used this episode to highlight one of the key points about successful dealings with the Japanese: 'If they ask for information which you know is at best marginally useful in a technical sense, just supply it. Anything to do with quality is sacrosanct. Respect it or else'.

Looking back over the 20 year relationship with NTC, the technical director recalls how at the outset 'it took ages to secure them as our agent in Japan, and a lot of unproductive time was spent in meetings'. In those days, the discussions were 'more like cross-examinations'. It had also taken time to get used to the formal approach to business preferred by the Japanese. But, eventually, he came to the conclusion that 'unrelaxed might be a better word for it than formal – especially with foreigners'. These days the meetings were markedly less formal than in the past, but his business partners were, as always, 'fiendishly well-prepared' for discussions. NTC also appear to have adapted a little to Western business ways: 'they actually have typed agendas'. The technical director describes his immediate NTC counterparts as 'very friendly'.

Slowly but surely he had come to accept the Japanese and their 'somewhat unusual ways of doing business', including the inordinate emphasis on business entertainment. In the course of twenty years of dealing in Japan he had been to every kind of establishment catering for the expense accounts of the big corporations: from sumptuous restaurants, where food is an aesthetic experience, to pokey bars with twittering hostesses. He had also allowed himself to be dragged into karaoke bars ('Don't ask me how many times I've done "I'll do it my way"!'). But it was all in a good cause: to get closer to NTC as his customer. Not only did he get to know much better his immediate counterparts, but also other NTC staff from other departments. It did not matter if these people had no direct connection with AngloChem's business. They all worked for NTC, his customer. So, meeting them, even socially, all helped to consolidate the total relationship.

PART C FACTORS INFLUENCING THE IMPACT OF PSYCHIC DISTANCE

As in the previous case study (Kamen Engineering Ltd.), the informant has seen personalization of commitment as central to relationship development. But he appeared to realize quite early in his dealings with NTC that 'total involvement', as he called it, was the single most important factor to the Japanese customer. This meant far more than making adaptations to the product and close cooperation over specifying its composition and performance. It meant ensuring that deliveries arrived on time; that technical service was prompt; and that queries and requests for information, no matter how abstruse, were dealt with efficiently. All this was the key to interdependence, and ultimately to the profitability and long-term security of the business to supplier and buyer.

'Total involvement' also required a very high preparedness to go along with the preferred Japanese way of doing business: attending lengthy meetings, complying with the customer's wishes to the greatest extent possible, offering solutions, sorting out mishaps fast. In the Japanese context involvement, from the supplier's point of view, means thinking through the consequences of things done and not done, and their impact on the customer and on any of his business relationships. This is second nature to Japanese firms. AngloChem, even if it did not articulate its relationship with NTC in these terms, appears to have developed forms of involvement which ensure that the NTC's other relationships are not compromised. But it has taken AngloChem several years to achieve this special form of closeness.

PART D KEY POINTS FOR MANAGING RELATIONSHIPS WITH JAPANESE CUSTOMERS

Rather like the case of Kamen, the relationship of AngloChem with its Japanese customer was strongly personalized. The term which AngloChem used to describe this relationship of some 20 years' standing was *total involvement*. Behind this orientation were a number of key actions and attitudes, focusing on these empirical insights:

- the building up of strong bonds of mutual trust takes many years
- reciprocity in relationships creates accommodating changes in Japanese attitudes and behaviour
- a willingness to ensure quality in all aspects of business performance
- a willingness to make product adaptations and innovations for Japanese customers.

Important learning points:

- Japanese customers can be loyal and therefore trusted
- taking to heart Japanese complaints and converting these into opportunities to improve service
- willingness to challenge one's own assumptions about the difficulties of doing business with Japanese customers.

Export relationships: the cultural asymmetries of interaction

When a Westerner meets a Japanese, many factors contribute to a sense of mutual unease. Each has his or her own prejudices to overcome, and there is a cultural gap so wide that many Westerners don't even know it is there.

Mark Zimmerman, *Dealing with the Japanese* (1985).

What is of the essence is the capacity to communicate oneself and one's business objectives within Japan's own terms of reference.

Herbert Glazer, quoted in: Paul Norbury and Geoffrey Bownas, *Business in Japan* (1974).

A t the end of each of the case studies in the last chapter we highlighted those factors which appeared to have a specific impact on psychic distance as a facet of the investigated relationships. It will be recalled that in Chapter 2, in line with the IMP Interaction Approach, psychic distance was held to be an element of atmosphere. In turn atmosphere was defined briefly as the sum of expectations which parties bring to a relationship, based on previous experience. It was then argued that psychic distance can be seen as an amalagam of cultural distance, social distance and trust.

The five case studies make it clear that psychic distance was a major factor impeding relationship development in three cases (Paper Industries Technology Ltd., BAS Ltd. and Delta Engineering Ltd.). In the two other cases (Kamen Engineering Ltd. and AngloChem Plc) psychic distance was a noticeable feature of the relationships at the outset, but had been reduced through a greater preparedness to commit themselves to their respective Japanese partners. In this chapter we shall make some generalizations about the atmosphere and psychic distance, using the material presented in the five case studies and data gathered on the interactions of four of the five other industrial firms who formed part of Abrahamsen's original sample (see Chapter 3, Methodology). The four companies concerned are: Northern Chemicals (industrial chemicals); W H Dykes Ltd. (organic chemicals); R. Parsley and Sons Ltd. (industrial doors and shutters); Maverick Cables Ltd. (electric cable).

We will then attempt to tease out those factors which appear to intensify first, cultural distance, then social distance and, finally, mistrust. It is conceded that studies of five relationships (or ten at best) can hardly claim to be representative of UK industrial firms and their involvements with Japan. On the other hand, we consider that their experiences of, and reactions to, dealing with Japanese business partners may in particular ways be reflected in other firms' experiences. We are also aware that we are only presenting the UK version of interactions and are making many assumptions about Japanese behaviour and attitudes.

ATMOSPHERE

The opening quotation by Mark Zimmerman (an excellent writer on Japanese business practices) provides a useful point of departure for understanding the nature of atmosphere in the UK-Japanese interactions presented in Chapter 3. Zimmerman highlights three factors which contribute to a difficult atmosphere for interactions involving Western and Japanese businessmen: a sense of mutual unease; Japanese and Western prejudices of each other; and the existence of a cultural gap of unsuspected complexity. In the case of PIT, BAS and Delta it is easy to imagine that their relationships to a marked degree were characterized by mutual unease, prejudices (which were possibly mutual) and misunderstandings of the impact of cultural factors on business development. In the other two cases involving Kamen and AngloChem, whose interactions were strikingly 'smooth' by comparison, we find that the negative impact of these three 'atmosphere-related' factors had not necessarily been eliminated, but weakened.

To account for this relatively sharp polarization in our sample, we must understand the significance of Zimmerman's three factors. But it is important to bear in mind, first, that they are by no means discrete categories, and, second, that they must be seen to be in the context of a very distinctive aspect of relationship atmosphere which appears to have considerable significance for Japanese customers: their *need* for the purchased product to protect their relationship with the end-users, their customers. This need will be presented as a fourth element of atmosphere. The 'discovery' of this need, based on a very tiny sample, is, as we shall see, borne out by Burgess in his investigation of the sub-contractor relationships. It may be the most significant marketing implication to arise from the two empirical studies forming the core of this book. First, though, we turn to Zimmerman's three points.

Mutual unease

The mutual unease that pervades Japanese encounters with Westerners (and all non-Japanese in general) is attributable to a multiplicity of causes. At the risk of considerable simplification, it is possible to isolate three main factors which contribute to the Japanese sense of unease: first, perceptions about unpredictability of Western business partners; second, a deep anxiety about themselves as cross-cultural communicators; and third, Japanese behaviour is conformist. The subtle – and sometimes not so subtle – means whereby this conformist behaviour is inculcated into Japanese people in every facet of their existence has been penetratingly discussed by the Dutch journalist, Karel van Wolferen, in his seminal book *The enigma of Japanese power*. In the home, at school, in university, each Japanese is trained to become a respectful member of society. This means learning how to behave: that is, to put it slightly idealistically, to know how to interact with all other Japanese to preserve outer harmony. Such 'harmonious' social interaction (the word 'harmonious' is in inverted commas because this quality is purely illusory) only works because practically every single Japanese understands how he or she must act in given circumstances to maintain appearances and to avoid causing offence to others.

The behaviour itself is governed by ritual and ceremony, and accompanied by elaborate forms of language. So important is correct behaviour that the graduate training programmes of major corporations provide instruction in the appropriate manner to present (and store) business cards and the correct use of language with senior members of the company, on the one hand, and customers, on the other (Holden, 1990). Female employees, who have the important job of welcoming company guests (i.e., customers) or speaking to them on the telephone, will have to learn 'extra-polite' forms of language and they may even have lessons in deportment. The essence of these processes is that each Japanese learns the preferred style of communication, which is based on a fondness for nuance and indirectness.

In the business sphere the stylized behaviour of businessmen conforms to accepted norms and standards. Non-Japanese, whether business people or not, stand out like sore thumbs in the company of Japanese. Their normal behaviour can variously strike the Japanese as odd, quaint, boorish, vulgar and uncivilized, especially on first encounters – and the Japanese, like everyone else, are strongly influenced by first impressions. The Westerner without previous experience of Japan is often unaware of how awkward it is for Japanese to adjust to him, especially as the Japanese instinct is, in Zimmerman's (1985) words, 'to find out as soon as possible where that person fits into his or her scheme of things': in other words, to establish the Westerner's relationship with his − occasionally, her − company.

When Japanese business people meet each other for the first time, they can go through the rituals of exchanging cards and greetings, the lesser-ranked interlocutor apologizing profusely for his ungracious intrusion and so forth. During this seemingly inconsequential social exchange, which is normally conducted by both parties with no sign of hurry or impatience, the two sides are scrutinizing each other's behaviour and reactions; assessing each other's sincerity; judging each other's value in terms of company prestige, the potential onerousness of obligations entered into, and opportunities for gaining introductions to influential people and organizations.

By contrast, dealing with non-Japanese can be irksome; the foreigners do not understand how to prepare the ground; they misunderstand the Japanese tendency to build a social relationship as a basis for business; they show the impatience that creates so many problems for the Japanese at the beginning of relationships. But, against that, the Japanese have enormous difficulty articulating their attitudes and intentions in English, their main language of international business communication (a matter that will receive more attention in due course).

Their innate fondness for indirectness − civilized behaviour in Japan − is often interpreted as evasion, untrustworthiness and even downright lying. Moreover, it seems impossible for those Japanese without extensive experience of dealing with foreigners in their own countries − in other words, the majority of Japanese in any walk of life − 'to develop any comprehension of the psychology of the English-speaking nations' (Christopher, 1984). The resultant 'communication gap' between Japanese and Westerners tends to be acutely felt by the former, and both underrated and misconceived by the latter. It is a perennial source of clashes, confusions and recriminations between Japan and the rest of the world at governmental level as well as at the level of business interactions. As we shall see later in this chapter, a major component of the communication gap is to do with the nature of the Japanese language.

Prejudices

Nearly 10 years ago a book came out with the intriguing title, *Japan versus Europe: A history of misunderstanding* (1983). It was written by Endymion Wilkinson, who had been head of economic and trade affairs of the EC Delegation in Tokyo 1974–1979. Wilkinson argued that many of the trade frictions between Europe and Japan – which 'festered like maggots in a rotting apple' – were in no small measure due to 'prejudice and outmoded images'. Wilkinson hoped that his book would help Japan and Europe understand the basis of their mutual wariness and antagonisms. The early 1980s were a boom time for the Japanese economy and a bad time for Europe, which was sensitive about falling behind America and Japan in the technological race.

Wilkinson said that the Japanese looked upon Europe as a mere 'cultural museum', and the prevailing view held by Europeans was that the Japanese were fanatical workaholics, welded into a huge techno-economic colossus, ominously called Japan Inc., with the whole monstrous creation being controlled from the bowels of MITI. In the elapsing years the Japanese presence in Europe has expanded markedly, but so has the European presence in Japan. With the massive exposure of Japan in all media, it may be the case that among European decision-makers (in the most general sense of the word) there is improved knowledge about Japan, but whether there has been a moderation of the wilder images of Japan is not certain. Interestingly, Wilkinson has just updated his book, which is no longer entitled *Japan versus Europe: A history of misunderstanding*, but *Japan versus the West: Image and reality*. This book, as the revised title implies, also embraces the fraught relationship between Japan and the USA. That one chapter is entitled 'Europe is dead, America is dying' is highly eloquent of Japan's unspoken attitudes towards Europe: a worn-out, inward-looking continent (but fortunately there are always the hard-working Germans to salvage some European honour).

There is still a persistent fear that Japanese businesss methods are underhand and that it is second nature to the Japanese to copy and improve both products and processes. Old images die hard, and they become part and parcel of the so-called cultural baggage that businesspeople, Western and Japanese, bring to their interactions. So, if a business plan fails, the Westerner can also say by way of twisted wish-fulfilment: 'I knew it would be a waste of time trying to do business with the Japanese. They are completely untrustworthy'. For their part, the Japanese can console themselves thus: 'Those foreigners never understand us. They refuse to accept the Japanese way of doing things even when we make every effort to be polite and sincere'. But whereas displays of politeness and sincerity send unambiguous messages among the Japanese, they not only fail to cross the cultural gulf, but also tend to reinforce Western suspicions of Japanese motives. This verse of Odgden Nash (quoted in: Emmott, 1990) distils very neatly the nature of this gulf:

> How courteous is the Japanese,
> He always says 'Excuse it please',
> He climbs into his neighbour's garden,
> And smiles and says 'I beg your pardon',
> He bows and grins a friendly grin,
> And calls his hungry family in.
> He grins, and bows a friendly bow,
> So sorry, this my garden now.'

Reprinted by permission of Curtis Brown Ltd. Copyright © 1935 by Ogden Nash.

Cultural gap

Zimmerman is not merely referring to the existence of a cultural gap, but alludes both to its all-pervading nature (the gap is 'so wide') and to its sub-liminal effect ('many Westerners don't even know it is there'). The customary view in all manner of management and marketing texts is to approach Japanese culture using traditional means: quoting one of the standard definitions of culture (of the 180 or so referred to in management literature), emphasizing that culture is something learned and shared by members of a society. This frequently entails a discussion of famous authorities on Japanese culture (Benedict and Nakane are almost *de rigueur*), with a liberal sprinkling of Japanese words for 1) characteristic phenomena relating to obligations, duties, face, consensus, private view and outward posture, and decision making, and 2) personal qualities admired by the Japanese, e.g., sincerity, forbearance, patience.

But there is a major problem in this approach to Japanese culture. It tends to overlook two dominant issues in Japanese life: 1) the Japanese highly-developed sense of cultural uniqueness, and 2) the Japanese language as the most potent defining feature of Japanese culture. To understand the Japanese culture of business interactions, it is vital to have a grasp of the influence of these two issues because both reveal much about Japanese attitudes to foreigners and attitudes to communicating with them.

First, the matter of uniqueness – a topic which has hardly been mentioned in the marketing literature on Japan. This is an issue that has attracted wide-ranging comment from important commentators outside the management domain (e.g., Dale, 1990; Reischauer, 1984; van Wolferen, 1989). Reischauer, a former US Ambassador to Japan and, until his death in 1990, America's foremost scholar of Japanese history and culture speaks of the clear-cut sharpness of 'the line between the "we" of the Japanese as a national group and the "they" of the rest of mankind'. Dambmann (1986), an illuminating German commentator, refers to a deep-seated Japanese need to keep themselves separate from other nations 'for their spiritual equilibrium' ('ihr seelisches Gleichgewicht').

Christopher (1984) mentions 'over-insistence on the unique nature of Japan'. This over-insistence, he points out, leads to 'self-delusion', not to mention farcical stupidity. Quite apart from outlandish claims to do with the uniqueness of the Japanese language, Japanese brain, Japanese management style and so on, we read that the Japanese islands have 'a unique geographical setting' (Hijirida and Yoshikawa, 1987). Holden recalls being utterly disconcerted by a Japanese who told him that Japan was unique for having been atom-bombed.

Dale (1990) makes the point that 'economic frictions with the outside world are reduced to unfortunate clashes in cultural style'. For his part, van Wolferen (1989) notes that 'the intermeshing relationships of the distribution system' and other factors 'that exclude foreigners from the market are sacrosanct cultural achievements'. In the same vein, the Japan

Embassy published a newsletter according to which Japanese investment in the UK 'forges deeper cultural links' (*Japan*, No. 485, 27 February 1990). Thus, the Japanese use the alleged uniqueness of their culture as a form of special pleading — and market protection. Behind all this is an assumption that foreigners are not really able to understand Japanese culture and, therefore, the special motives which infuse Japanese economic endeavour.

A major component of the culture gap is the Japanese language. But the crux of the issue is not the undeniable difficulty of the Japanese language for foreigners to learn (and, incidentally for the Japanese themselves), but the mythology that the Japanese have created about their language: it is revered as a unique endowment of an equally unique race (see Miller, 1977 and 1982; Dale, 1990), as a mystical repository of Japanese values. The claim that 'it possesses a "spirit" unlike any in any other language' (van Wolferen, 1989) is, as Dale (1990) points out 'a reflex of the principle that what is uniquely Japanese is inapprehensible to foreigners'. Consequently, according to the mythology, no matter how hard a foreigner attempts to learn the Japanese language, he is intellectually and intuitively incapable of entering the thought-world of the Japanese.

In case it is thought that there is some exaggeration on these points, it has been a widely-held experience of many foreign students of Japanese that they are complimented for the excellence of their Japanese for saying 'konnichi wa' (good day/hallo) or for putting a simple sentence together in Japanese; or, when they address Japanese people in their own language, realizing that the Japanese are not hearing Japanese (see Miller, 1982; Holden, 1983; Reischauer, 1984; Zimmerman, 1985). Holden once used a solitary Japanese word in a sentence in English directed to an English-speaking Japanese scientist. He was amazed to be informed that he had 'a very good knowledge of Japanese' — what if he had used two Japanese words! In the light of these language attitudes, Miller (1982) has formulated the 'Law of Inverse Returns', according to which 'the better you get at the language, the less credit you are given for your achievements; the more fluently you speak it, the less your hard-won skills will do for you in the way of making friends and impressing people'. Miller notes that this law applies only to Americans and Europeans '... Koreans, Chinese, South-

East Asians, even Indians are exempt from the curious provisions of the law'.

The point is, we are not talking about a 'normal' language barrier. Dale (1990) speaks of 'a semantic bamboo curtain between Japan and the outside world'. Reischauer (1984) describes the Japanese language as 'a major problem' in Japan's international relationships. It is undeniably the most complex language barrier in the industrial advanced world: defining the 'unique' Japanese thought-world, perpetuating the sharp line between the Japanese and all other nations, and acting as 'the very crucible of [Japanese] identity'. Thus, the Japanese language is a major facet of cultural distance: it imposes severe limits on our capacity to understand 'the norms, values, or working methods' (Ford, 1980) of Japanese business partners and of their companies. But the Japanese language is also a major element in social distance, as we shall see presently.

The product

In the preceding paragraphs we looked at atmosphere from three perspectives: mutual unease, prejudices and cultural gap. We now turn to the identified fourth element: the role of the product in the exchange process. At first glance the inclusion of product under atmosphere has no logic, until it is grasped that in Japanese eyes products have symbolic value. The point is this: whenever a Japanese company purchases products for use by their customers in turn, the Japanese company envisages those products not just in terms of satisfying the end-user's needs; it is at least as much concerned with the consequences that the supply of this product will have for the relationship with the end-user. All this is nerve-racking enough when the original supplier is Japanese, but with foreign suppliers the Japanese customer forever fears the twin spectre of late delivery and inferior quality.

Thus the product in exchanges, as far as Japanese purchasers are concerned, is much more than the so-called augmented product of Western marketing experts — the idea that the customer buys products for benefits and satisfactions as well as functional features. In Japan, the important thing about products is that they *protect* relationships between the final purchaser and the immediate supplier (who does not have to be the manufacturer).

The protection of relationships is of paramount importance in all Japanese business life. When Japanese companies sense that the involvement of a foreign supplier is going to adversely affect the integrity of any of their relationships, the way ahead for the foreign company will be arduous, if not completely blocked. Thus Japanese perceptions of a product in this particular respect, whether based on anticipation or actual experience, are a significant element in what might be termed 'the atmosphere landscape', the asymmetrically perceived terrain of interaction and involvement.

Ensuring the product, *in this expanded, talismanic sense,* is just right for the end-user is a central preoccupation of the Japanese purchaser; it is very time-consuming (a word the UK suppliers frequently applied to their business discussions), and it is the motivation for Japanese requests for both 'useless' information and product modifications.

Cultural distance, social distance and mistrust

The purpose of the above extended section on atmosphere landscape was to provide additional clues for understanding the nature of cultural differences and their effect on the development of relationships between the UK firms and their Japanese customers. Every single one commented on cultural differences as having a major impact on the overall atmosphere of the interactions. All five companies reacted in their own particular way to the demands and tensions associated with the atmosphere landscape, and it was noticeable that only two of the five firms (Kamen and AngloChem) appeared to be successfully keeping the psychic distance within manageable proportions.

Bearing in mind the general points about atmosphere landscape, we turn again to the five firms' experiences and perceptions of doing business in Japan. The main purpose is to isolate factors associated with the three elements of psychic distance: cultural distance, social distance and mistrust. However, because in Chapter 3 and the first few pages of this chapter the two types of distance have received a reasonable amount of direct and indirect treatment, our overriding concern will be with the matter of mistrust.

In three of the cases (PIT, BAS and Delta) mistrust emerged, but for different reasons, as a potent factor in the interactions. In the case of AngloChem, mistrust had been a significant factor for the first few years of the relationship. Only Kamen appeared to have trusted its Japanese counterpart from the beginning; four of the other five companies interviewed by Abrahamsen in the main were worried about the alleged lack of trustworthiness of their Japanese business partners. Some of their perceptions and reactions will be noted. In the following discussion of cultural distance, social distance and mistrust, we shall highlight broad clusters of factors which appear, on the one hand, to reinforce and, on the other, to attenuate the effect of each of the factors.

Cultural distance: the contributory factors

Ford (1990) defines cultural distance as the 'degree to which norms, values or working methods between two companies differ because of their separate national characteristics'. This definition has been usefully augmented by Swift (1990), who sees cultural difference as 'the outcome of the difference in culture between buyer and seller; the more "alien" the other culture appears to each participant, the greater the cultural distance between the two'.

Careful analysis of the respondents' stated experiences and perceptions of doing business in Japan clearly suggests that cultural differences were universally considered to have a major impact on interactions and relationship development. However, it is the social level of interaction where these differences become most sharply felt, played out, and either neutralized or intensified. As the section below on social distance makes clear, most firms had enormous problems coping with Japanese culture as mediated through the actions of their Japanese counterparts.

But looking at culture as an abstraction, eight companies out of the full sample of ten companies lacked a clear appreciation of the nature of Japanese companies as culturally ordained institutions pursuing social and economic objectives. This explains why most respondents could neither understand the decision-making procedures nor account for the Japanese preoccupation with 'secrecy'. Some respondents referred to Japanese group-orientation ('collectivism' was one informant's description) as something they disapproved of; they did not seem to see this as a facet of Japanese company organization that required them to modify their business approach.

But perhaps the most telling finding from the sample was that those firms who assumed, either out of laziness, unprofessionalism or sheer boorishness, that Japan could be approached like other export markets were those who also found the market to be most closed, Japanese companies to be the least responsive, and Japanese businessmen to be the least trustworthy. The situation was neatly summed up by the export manager of W H Dykes Ltd., who had been trying in vain since 1986 to sort out their 'increasingly very bad' relationship with their customer, a major Japanese trading house. Dykes's managing director was continually exasperated by 'the distance from the market, Japanese culture, local loyalties and unclear relationships'.

Cultural distance: the attenuating factors

Two factors emerged as having a significant impact on lessening the impact of cultural distance. The first was sheer experience of doing business in Japan, combined with a determination not to allow cultural differences or other factors to impede business development perceived to be mutually beneficial. This qualification of experience is important; as it will be recalled, the chairman of PIT had read a good deal about Japanese history and culture, but his overriding fear was that his customer would make off with this technology.

The second attenuating factor, derived from the first, concerned cultural stereotypes. In the sample's responses it is clear that greater experience brought modified, generally more positive, images of the Japanese. The companies who had more difficulty developing relationships were those who stressed that it was not easy to get along with the Japanese ('getting along with' seems to be a very important need of British businesspeople). They perceived the Japanese to be secretive, untrustworthy and inscrutable as well as verbally vague and unclear. These respondents constituted five out of the sample of ten companies, and of these only one had gone to 'great lengths' to seek advice – from, say, the DTI's Exports to Japan Unit – or to brief themselves systematically on approaching the Japanese market and dealing with the Japanese.

In other words, these firms tended to retain the traditional stereotypes. The firms who had developed more sophisticated business relationships found the Japanese to be loyal to suppliers (even if they did not fully appreciate supplier problems), efficient in handling their side of the relationship, and friendly and cooperative in their dealings.

Social distance: the contributory factors

Social distance is concerned with factors which impede relationships at the personal level of interaction through unfamiliarity with each other's way of working (Ford, 1980).

Eight of the ten companies investigated cited a number of Japanese business practices with which they were unfamiliar and to which, with varying degrees of commitment and success, they tried to accommodate themselves. These practices – 'ludicrous customs', according to the BAS representative – included the formality of business discussions, the ritual associated with exchanges of business cards, and the secrecy which surrounded information about their company and business relationships inside Japan. Some informants were also taken unawares by the high degree of preparedness of the Japanese when approaching business discussions. This can be seen as a factor in social distance, as the implied lack of preparation by the UK companies may have been a corresponding shock to their Japanese counterparts.

Various respondents referred to the ritual associated with the presentation of business cards, the practice of gift-giving, the inordinate length of business discussions, the inexpressiveness of Japanese faces and absence of gestures, and the mysteries of decision-making. Two companies described themselves as having been 'cross-examined' by Japanese companies in their bid to become suppliers. All companies referred to language problems as a factor that impeded the development of closeness; only one respondent, the BAS manager, considered this to be a very serious issue, and the contracts manager of Kamen, who had shown himself to be an astute business partner of the Japanese, had found language problems to be 'acute'. In the section on cultural gap the language barrier was presented as a complex phenomenon. We need to say a few words about the language barrier at the interpersonal level of contact.

In every investigated interaction, English was the language used in all business communication. The Japanese (for reasons alluded to above) expect to speak English with foreign businessmen. But this raises two complex problems. First, the Japanese find it immensely difficult to speak and understand English, despite years of language education in school and university and within the company (Holden, 1989). Foreigners, especially perhaps UK and US businessmen, for whom foreign language proficiency and the pains to achieve it are not a personal experience, tend not to notice this and fail to modify their speech – its content and speed of delivery – accordingly.

The second point is that, when they speak English, the Japanese in effect 'think in Japanese'. The result is not just well-intentioned, often impenetrable English, but a hybrid lingo called 'Japlish', in which the English language is subordinated to the Japanese social requirement of preserving and maintaining harmonious relationships. Japlish, then, is a form of English created by the Japanese for interaction with foreigners to avoid confrontation. But the English language does not lend itself naturally to the Japanese long-ingrained penchant for polite evasion and oblique reference and the resulting Japanese-style English has an unfortunate way of sending out wrong signals – and, where wariness exists in a relationship, this may turn to mistrust and scepticism.

Social distance: the attenuating factors

The first requirement for reducing the effects of social distance is to accept that any kind of exasperation with the Japanese will be interpreted by them as impatience, which is considered in Japan to be both a sign of weakness and bad manners. Zimmerman (1985) is quite right to caution Western businessmen on the 'evils' of impatience: 'The mistakes most commonly made by Westerners when they first begin dealing with the Japanese all arise from impatience'. Another American, Robert Christopher (1984) supplies the antidote in a nutshell: 'The things to cultivate are patience, persistence, a knack for indirection, an ear for nuance – and a sharp eye for the occasional moving finger.' This tiny gesture is Japanese body language for: 'This discussion is a total waste of time'. Another give-away gesture, and one much harder to detect, is the glaze that comes over the Japanese eye when interest has evaporated.

As for the language issues, Zimmerman (1985) has sound advice (that is emphasized in his book): *one must speak clear, slower-than-normal, extraprecise English when speaking to a Japanese*. Zimmerman throws in for good measure pertinent advice to those who have not yet mastered the art of concentrated listening in their dealings with Japanese businessmen: *keep your mouth shut*. A further factor which helps to reduce social distance is the recognition that interactions with a Japanese company have several aspects that fall outside Western business experience and assumptions (for example, the role of the product as a facet of atmosphere). At the interpersonal level of interaction it is as well to be aware that personal behaviour – from flashes of impatience (bad sign) to neatness of appearance (good sign) – tend to symbolize for the Japanese the competence, capability and commitment of foreign suppliers. This is why the choice of person to head up a foreign supplier's relationships with Japan is so important. This point will be considered further when we look at factors to reduce mistrust.

Mistrust: the contributory factors

The most-mentioned factor concerning the UK perceptions of Japanese trustworthiness related to the Japanese penchant for secrecy – a source of major need uncertainty. In the case of PIT the perceived untrustworthiness was related to the UK firm's assumption that its business partner,

Yamagushi, was trying to obtain PIT technology in order eventually to produce a directly competitive product line. Thus PIT saw its days as a supplier to the Japanese market as being numbered. A similar situation faced R. Parsley and Sons, who described their Japanese customer as 'sharks' in their unrelenting probing for technical information.

There were also references to the Japanese reluctance to impart information about end-users or the state of the market in Japan. This is a knotty problem for three main reasons; first, as noted in the discussion about social distance, language difficulties have a way of impeding trust; second, British firms appear to regard even general business information from customers as normal business practice (this is borne out by the extensive study by Turnbull and Cunningham (1981)); third, it seems to be psychologically impossible for a Japanese firm to pass on 'insider information', even of seemingly non-confidential nature, to an outsider – perhaps especially a foreign one.

The last two points tend to put UK and Japanese firms on a potential collision course. In the case of PIT it is noticeable that to maintain a market position through Yamagushi the UK firm has provided its Japanese customer with certain technical particulars. This should not be seen as naive, but more a reflection of British firms' tendency to be reasonably open. The fact that Japanese firms are not correspondingly open gives rise to the all too familiar complaint that information between Japan and other companies tends to go West to East. One difficulty that a Japanese firm has about revealing information about firms in its network is it cannot understand why a foreign company actually needs it. The argument would go something like this: if the Japanese firm is the sole importer for a foreign firm, is taking the risk of supplying foreign products to its customers, and is vouching *vis-à-vis* these customers for quality, reliability and performance, why should the foreign firm need information?

In this line of thinking there is a subliminal assumption that it is also not necessary for 'too many' foreigners to be visible in particular market sectors. Foreigners by their nature can all too readily disrupt the delicate system of checks and balances between Japanese business collaborators. The Japanese attitude is: keep the foreigners at bay. In any case, foreigners cannot begin to understand the intricate, convoluted nature of Japanese business networks – another good reason for not giving them information which is going to be useless.

The thinking here is strongly reminiscent of the experiences of the very few Dutch traders in Japan in the first half of the nineteenth century, one of whom was not permitted to keep his wife and child with him. As noted by von Siebold (1841/1981) with his own emphasis: 'This severity of exclusion is not directed specially against Hollanders, or even foreign *women*, but against all persons who are not *positively necessary to carrying on the trade*. The general principle of the Japanese is, that no-one must enter their country *without cause*'.

Another source of mistrust stems from Japanese perceptions about the 'inferior quality' of Western products, management systems and manufacturing techniques. Not only are the Japanese convinced that they are paramount in these areas, but the rest of the world is also telling them that this is indeed the case. Unless there is good reason, it is much safer to stay with, and put pressure on, Japanese suppliers. Then, as implied in the section on the product above, the suppliers misunderstand the way in which the customers see the products, i.e., as protectors of other, all-Japanese relationships. The nature of the Japanese 'product-orientation', combined with their own misgivings about the reliability of foreign supplies, certainly accounts for their perceived lack of cooperativeness and occasional pressing for price concessions.

Mistrust: the attenuating factors

In descriptions of their very first encounters with Europeans in the middle of the sixteenth century (see Boxer, 1974; Cooper, 1981), one is continually struck by the remarkable constancy of Japanese behaviour and attitudes. Records from the sixteenth century attest to Japanese technological expertise, their skill in reproducing (and adapting) foreign artefacts, their hankering after new things, their intelligence, their exquisite refinement of manners and speech – and their adroitness in dissembling.

So, when it comes to the well-known Japanese tendency to assimilate knowledge, to copy and adapt, firms dealing with contemporary Japan cannot expect the Japanese to renounce this historically ingrained characteristic. Nor can they expect the Japanese to 'suddenly' provide information on customers and markets. For reasons explained above, that would also be tantamount to requiring the leopard to change its spots.

Despite this, Japanese firms can be open. Consider this example concerning Maverick Cables, a company in Abrahamsen's original sample, who had a somewhat disarming experience on their very first encounter with their Japanese customer: a senior manager chose this occasion to give them a copy of a report on the Japanese cable market prepared by their previous supplier from the US. Subsequently Maverick Cables described its Japanese customer as 'trustworthy, loyal business partners, friendly but secretive'. But the episode about handing over the previous supplier's market report is revealing. This gesture suggests that the information was no longer considered 'secret', because the relationship with its purveyor − a US, i.e., a non-Japanese company   had ceased to exist.

But that was an unusual occurrence. So, bearing in mind the more normal Japanese mistrust of foreigners, what remedies are available to Western firms? In our case studies two very interesting and contrasting approaches proved successful. In the first case, that of AngloChem, the company took a long-term view of business development and concentrated on modifying its products to suit its customer and supplying products of a consistently high standard. The second approach, exemplified by Kamen, was to work towards mutual commitment − at all stages the contracts manager trusting rather than mistrusting.

In passing, we should mention the experience of another company in Abrahamsen's original sample, Northern Chemicals Ltd. Since 1986 this company has been selling industrial chemicals for use in tyre production to its main customer, Nippon Chemicals Inc. After a hesitant beginning, when Nippon Chemicals vacillated between Northern Chemicals and a local supplier (an experience which still haunts the UK firm), a generally cooperative relationship blossomed. For its part Northern Chemicals overhauled its quality control procedures to meet Nippon Chemicals' requirements. 'Once the breakthrough had been made', commented the managing director, 'the most important factor was improving – not just maintaining – quality of service and products'. This display of commitment was central to business development; it also made Nippon Chemicals more tolerant of the UK firm's occasional inability to keep its delivery schedules – an otherwise clear indicator to Japanese companies of the untrustworthiness of foreign suppliers.

It should not escape our notice that the representatives of Delta and Kamen personalized to a high degree the relationships and the resulting commitments. This bears out the conviction that 'success in Japan (once you have grasped the strategy) is the man you send out to represent you. This person does not need to understand the Japanese language, but he does need to understand the Japanese people' (Tajima, in: Norbury and Bownas, 1974). This person needs, above all else, intelligence, persistence and tact. As a former US Ambassador wisely observed: 'if you try to accommodate the Japanese in matters of style, they will usually try to accommodate you in matters of substance'.

PSYCHIC DISTANCE AND JAPAN: MARKETING IMPLICATIONS

The device of 'disaggregating' psychic distance into the component elements of cultural distance, social distance and trust/mistrust has been useful in throwing light on the interactions of a cross-section of UK exporters of industrial and technical goods with their main (and in some cases, their only) Japanese customer. What emerges from the analysis is that a marketing approach that fails to take account of certain highly unusual features of the Japanese market may backfire, and for reasons that may easily elude both the person sent to Japan and his company in the UK. The case studies and their analysis in terms of psychic distance cannot offer more than a partial guide to firms seeking to commence or expand business with Japan. With luck, they offer firms (and others) ideas (and cautionary tales) on a matter completely neglected in the marketing literature on Japan: the honing of a business approach to the Japanese market using psychological insights.

From our studies there are three key 'marketing-psychological' implications. First, the striking disparity between the high state of preparedness of Japanese business partners and that of UK suppliers suggests to the Japanese a total lack of professionalism, a lack of what they call sincerity (i.e., a demonstrated willingness to think through the consequences of any involvement, to strive for harmony in the relationship, and to fulfil obligations without shirking).

The second implication concerns the person who handles the relationship with the Japanese customers. He needs, as noted above, several key personal attributes: intelligence, persistence, and tact. It seems too that a capacity to personalize the relationship (a colossal personal commitment, incidentally) is a major attribute. Finally, if it is not asking too much of this rare person, the ability – and willingness – to speak English carefully and patiently with Japanese partners (going over the same points again and again) is a wonderfully advantageous professional skill. We are calling this key person 'the Japan interfacer' and we will have more to say about this role in Chapter 9.

The third implication, discussed at some length, is the importance of looking at products in exchanges as an element of relationship atmosphere. The traditional Western marketing view that products deliver benefits has only limited applicability in Japan. The view we are presenting is that the foreign supplier must understand that his product serves a crucially important purpose: that of protecting the Japanese customer's relationship with the end-user. It is essential to grasp that the Japanese customer's desire to protect this relationship (and all others) is a major business need.

As noted earlier, this unusual form of product orientation also proved to be a major business need of Japanese manufacturing subsidiaries in the UK in their relationships with British subcontractors. We now direct our attention to these relationships. Needless to say, the UK-based Japanese industrial customer cannot be presented as a culturally homogeneous entity. He must be seen a cultural hybrid, a fusion of British and Japanese styles and influences which do not necessarily complement each other.

PART 3

The geometry of subcontractor relationships: UK and Japanese perspectives

Local components are our most serious problem in manufacturing in the UK.

Mr T. Negishi, Director Europe, Electronics Industries Association of Japan. Quoted in: Malcolm Trevor and Ian Christie, *Manufacturers in Britain and Japan: Competitiveness and growth of the small firm.*

They [the Japanese] are peculiarly sensitive to the smell of decay, however well screened; and they will strike at an enemy whose core appears to betray a lack of firmness.

Kurt Singer, *Mirror, sword and jewel* (1989).

In Chapters 3 and 4 we were concerned with describing and analysing the relationships of UK suppliers of technical products to the Japanese market. We used the IMP Interaction Approach, concentrating on the atmosphere of relationships and on the impact of psychic distance. We are now going to apply the same approach, again with case studies, to a different category of UK supplier relationships with Japanese companies; the difference being that the customers are UK-based manufacturing subsidiaries of Japanese multinational corporations. This means, of course, that the atmosphere landscape is not the same as that which characterized the export relationships. One immediate difference is that the suppliers are operating on their own territory. Another, as we shall find, is that the purchasing of components and other engineering supplies is normally handled by UK managers; in other words, not by Japanese personnel. Thus we are concerned with selling to Japanese companies, but not to Japanese personnel.

This, however, is not to say that the suppliers necessarily approach their UK-based Japanese customers as if they were 'just like any other UK firm' or that the purchasing managers perform their functions without being influenced by Japanese attitudes. In fact the evidence now available, and we review some of it presently, is that UK supplier firms are finding it necessary to modify their approach because the purchasing managers are insisting on unusually high levels of product quality and on unusually detailed technical information. Moreover, the Japanese firms are showing a marked preference for developing relationships with suppliers who make the grade. This of course is standard practice in Japan, as we shall see presently; but it is also a practice that Marks and Spencer, for example, have applied for many years. The preference for developing subcontractor relationships stems from the simple recognition that the major customer, with its enormous purchasing power, can guarantee the subcontractor long-term business provided that the latter satisfies all the requirements covering quality, performance, delivery and service. Under the 'rules' of this system major customers in effect reduce their supplier base and are also in a very strong position to secure favourable prices. The 'survival-of-the-fittest' element in these practices have been lost on no one, and the wider acceptance of the benefits of focused subcontractor development in manufacturing industry has been a direct result of the impact of Japanese quality management practices.

Gone are the days in the UK car industry, for example, when the big manufacturers would play off a multiplicity of suppliers against each other, with price being sacrificed for quality. In fact the impact has been so great that academics now write about the Japanization of British industry, and a recent conference held in striking distance of the Toyota car plant was named 'Japan and the regeneration of British industry' (*Anglo Japanese Journal*, May–August 1991). The net effect of focusing attention on the impact of 'Japanese-style' subcontractor development has been to observe the phenomenon in terms of British industrial competitiveness and its relative decline. In the next chapter we examine in detail the experiences of five UK industrial suppliers involved as subcontractors to UK-based Japanese manufacturers. In order to compare and contrast these experiences with the export relationships described and analysed earlier in this book, the IMP Interaction Approach will be used and, as before, we are especially interested in relationship atmosphere and the impact of psychic distance.

To put the case studies in context, the remainder of this chapter will deal with the following topics: 1) the UK subcontractor environment and the position of the manufacturing supply-base in terms of UK industrial competitiveness; 2) the scale of Japanese manufacturing investment in the UK; 3) an introduction to Japanese manufacturing techniques and concepts of quality management; 4) a characterization of subcontractor relationships in Japan; 5) a review of three studies on Japanese management of subcontractor relationships in the UK. Topics 3) and 4) are included in order to make clear the fundamental differences of the Japanese concepts of manufacturing and the role of subcontractors in Japan.

BRITISH MANUFACTURING SUPPLY-BASE COMPETITIVENESS

For a number of years it has been propounded that the decline in competitiveness of British industry is fundamentally due to non-cost factors. Factors such as product quality, delivery performance, new product development and customer service have been cited as more responsible for the declining UK share of world markets than the price of British products. The influential *Finneston Report* (1980) on the state of the engineering profession noted that: 'Customers' evaluations of value-for-money from manufactured products ... and capital goods have increasingly stressed the relative importance of non-price factors based upon the expected total cost of the purchase over its useable life'.

A study by Turnbull (1984) of the European view of British suppliers' competence found that UK firms were rated very poorly on three key non-price factors – delivery performance, product quality and new product technology. At the same time Shipley (1984) conducted a study of supplier selection criteria for industrial goods. The criteria cited as the most important in component sourcing were quality, delivery speed and reliability, specification fulfilment and price. These and other studies have consistently identified non-price factors as fundamental to UK suppliers' loss of competitiveness.

This poor showing, not just by the component suppliers but also by OEMs (original equipment manufacturers), was a major contributory factor in the relative decline of the UK manufacturing base, thereby bringing chronic unemployment, negatively affecting the UK's balance of payments position and generally weakening international competitiveness. This conclusion of the ICC 1982 Business Ratio Report as quoted in Burgess (1991) on the state of vehicle component suppliers did not mince its words: 'There is no doubt that the performance of the UK motor components sector has been horrific and has mirrored, if not led, the decline in industrial output in this country'.

Another commentator (Gooding, 1987) estimated that the automobile supply industry alone lost over 126 000 jobs from 1979 to 1983, quoting the Manufacturing Director of the Rover Group who stated he could no longer source a whole range of components in the UK: gas filled suspension struts, self-levelling suspension units, fuel injectors, electric seat slides, seat belt webbing, aerials and even mirror glass.

The erosion of the UK's supply-base not only brings unemployment and its attendant social ills; it can also implicitly affect the ability of UK OEMs to manufacture high quality, technologically-advanced products. In

other words, the weakening of the supply-base contributes to losses of efficiency by the major manufacturers. As Carr (1990) notes, with specific reference to the car industry: 'Since OE (original equipment) components
represent about 55 per cent of most European vehicle assemblers' costs,
the competitive fortunes of UK assemblers and their suppliers are highly
interdependent'.

Over the years a number of panaceas have been proposed to improve
the performance of UK firms with respect to non-price factors. The panaceas
have included recommendations on: workforce flexibility, automation of
production, better marketing of products, and smoother labour relations,
fiscal policies relating to deflation and investment levels. By the mid-1980s
a radically unexpected form of solution materialized: Japan. In the words
of Illidge (1987): 'The search for remedies to improve the efficiency of British
industry has led to Japan being studied as a model for potential economic
regeneration'.

A number of interrelated factors came into play. First, Japanese firms
were widely recognized for their outstanding quality products, rapid development cycle time, and unique approach to vendor relationships
(Abbeglen and Stalk 1985), all areas where UK firms in general were weak.
Second, the influx of Japanese investment into the UK was already exert-
ing a powerful influence throughout the general manufacturing sector. One
of their conspicuous successes was in striking deals with British trades
unions and markedly raising worker productivity. As the UK-based Japanese
companies introduced their latest ideas, technology and quality control,
no major manufacturer could ignore these transformations. The Japanese
ideas appeared to be working, and with British workforces. So Japanese
firms, as well as conferring economic benefits on a particular region and
offering steady business to the supply industry, were beginning to be seen
as a kind of industrial role model.

In order to appreciate the almost revolutionary impact of Japanese
philosophies and practices on the supply industry, we need to say a few
words about traditional relations between major manufacturers and their
subcontractors. A DTI report, published in 1988, characterized these relations in just one word: 'adversarial'. The main strategy of OEMs was one

of price minimization and multi-sourcing. This meant that major component users played off one subcontractor against another, provided minimal amounts of information and actively encouraged price cutting in the supply-base. By these means the supply industry is kept weak and is in perpetual fear of losing bulk orders to rivals who undercut them.

It goes without saying that price is an important factor and that a typical assembly-based OEM's manufacturing costs are heavily affected by the price of bought-in components from vendors. Horn et al. (1987) estimate that up to 80 per cent of manufacturing costs and 50 per cent of the sale price of a finished product are accounted for by these bought-in parts. Consequently it would appear to be perfectly rational for the OEM to employ a purchasing policy of component price minimization, and as a result significantly reduce transaction costs. But a consequence of these 'rational', but aggressively pursued, strategies has been that many UK suppliers tend to supply only standardized components, as there is less and less incentive to develop non-standard specializations, invest in newer technology or take on or train a workforce with quality skills. Inevitably, OEM-supplier relationships have come to be dominated by spot-contracting, which refers to the opportunistic practice of placing short-term, discreet and frequently-altered orders (Williamson, 1979).

Not surprisingly, supplier firms have tended to avoid being dependent upon, or tied to, one main customer. Indeed, dependence on one main customer is not just bad management on the part of suppliers, it can be suicidal. The pervading atmosphere of mistrust has resulted in supplier cynicism *vis-à-vis* its customers and low priority being given to component quality and delivery performance. This state of affairs has prompted Horn et al. (1987) to point out that indifferent supplier performance inevitably leads to manufacturer inefficiencies which 'far outweigh the cost advantage' theoretically gained from aggressive cost-minimization strategies.

Recognition of the negative consequences of these strategies both for the supply-base and the OEMs has led to an awareness of the strategic importance of the supply function to general industrial competitiveness. With this in mind, Macbeth and Ferguson (1990), for example, have been urging major manufacturers to revise their attitudes towards suppliers, encouraging them to see purchasing not as a mechanism for getting components at the cheapest price, but as 'strategic supply chain management'. Several major manufacturing corporations are now taking a more enlightened view of their relationships with suppliers. But this is not due to a sudden inrush of noble sentiment about the supply-base; they were strongly influenced by the awesome global performance of Japanese manufacturing companies, whose relationships with subcontractors are based on 'greater mutuality and equality of bargaining strength' (Dore, 1986).

JAPANESE MANUFACTURING INVESTMENT IN THE UK

In January 1990, according to JETRO (Japanese External Trade Organization), there were 529 Japanese manufacturing firms operating in the EC, of which 132 were sited in the UK. Although the manufacturing sector accounts for less than 15 per cent of the total Japanese manufacturing investment in the UK, the country has received 30.1 per cent of the total manufacturing investment in the whole of the EC. Astonishingly, perhaps, this investment in the manufacturing sector amounts to less than two per cent of the total Japanese investment in the UK.

UK-based Japanese manufacturers are predominantly in three sectors: cars, electric and electronic consumer goods, and computer-related manufactures. The heaviest sectoral investment is associated with the three car makers, Honda, Nissan and Toyota, who are estimated to have introduced around £1.8bn worth of investment in the UK. For its part, Toyota has invested £840m in the UK; £700m in an assembly plant at Burnaston, Derbyshire, and £140m in an engine building factory at Shotton. It has been estimated that the UK supply-base could eventually provide the main Toyota plant with 60−70 per cent of its component requirements; this suggests £420m of business to the UK's hard-hit automotive component sector.

Nissan is now probably sourcing over 70 per cent of its components from local suppliers. Its supply-base comprises about 170 supply companies throughout the EC, of whom 120 are British. It is estimated that these UK firms share the estimated Nissan annual spend of £440m on components (*Engineer*, 5 July 1990). Within five years the UK-based Japanese car makers will produce around 600 000 cars, half of them destined for export (even now Nissan exports more than 40 per cent of their production). Nissan, for example, aims to quadruple annual output to 400 000 vehicles by the end of the decade − more than Rover and Vauxhall, and on a par with Ford.

Komatsu, who manufacture earth-moving equipment, is believed to obtain much of its annual component requirement, estimated to be worth £44m annually to EC firms, from UK sources (*Engineer*, 31 August 1989). Fujitsu, the computer giant, who already has a £400m semi-conductor plant in Newton Aycliffe, bought up 80 per cent of ICL in July 1990 for £750m. It is no exaggeration to say that the UK computer industry will never be the same again. Indeed it is unlikely that UK industry as a whole will ever be the same again, such is the extent of Japanese investment, bringing with it thousands of jobs often in depressed regions. But beyond that there has been the Japanese influence on concepts of sourcing, quality management and manufacturing, concepts increasingly being seen as vital elements of Japan's 'super-competitiveness'.

JAPANESE MANUFACTURING TECHNIQUES

British-based Japanese manufacturers use a combination of techniques for improving efficiency of production and maintaining (and raising) product quality. However, it would be mistaken to see them as narrowly focused around production. The Japanese techniques, with the philosophies that underlie them, relate directly to the role of suppliers and the quality of their output, the flow of materials through the plant, the human and non-human organizational aspects of production proper, and the delivery of the final products. The Japanese tend to look upon these highly complex activities as integrated; the systems and subsystems they evolve entail close cooperation with subcontractors, highly sophisticated quality control procedures, and a powerful impulse to make the whole process as cost-efficient as possible – without falling into the black hole of price minimization.

The most commonly known techniques are total quality management (TQM) and just-in-time (JIT) production (see Schonberger, 1982 and 1985; Sugimori et al., 1977). There is also the concept of continuous improvement (which is sometimes propagated under the Japanese word 'kaizen'; see Imai, 1986), which in the UK is most strongly associated with the Nissan approach to quality management. TQM involves statistical process control (SPC) and its purpose is to achieve zero defect (ZD) production within a company environment totally committed to quality in all aspects of performance. JIT, in nutshell, is 'a theory of manufacturing in which parts [arrive] just in time to be part of the final assembly' (Halberstam, 1986).

This system, perfected by Toyota in Japan, requires close coordination between OEMs and their suppliers, whose product quality and delivery performance are of critical importance. JIT can only operate if reliable, high quality component supplies are available to major manufacturers and can be delivered frequently and in small batches. Iizuka and Monden (1988) state that JIT 'can yield its maximum effect only when adopted as a total system in which suppliers are involved'. This means, as Harrison and Voss (1989) point out, that suppliers themselves must adopt TQM policies, often utilizing statistical process control (SPC) and aiming for zero defect production (ZD) to be capable of JIT supply. In the case of kaizen, as we shall see in Chapter 6, this technique can only work if the supplier is willing and able to improve methods of working in close cooperation with the customer.

Such philosophies are, needless to say, a far cry from the traditional practices in the UK described earlier. Although the techniques themselves are important, perhaps the most fundamental effect of Japanese manufacturing techniques is in challenging traditional Western attitudes to production and quality management. As Imai (1986) notes, the differences in the Japanese approach contrast the Japanese 'process-orientated way of thinking' with Western 'innovation-and results-orientated thinking'.

In Chapter 6 we shall be considering at length five interactions involving

UK subcontractors and major UK-based manufacturers. The above, very brief, commentary makes it clear that Japanese firms have a radically different concept of subcontractor relationships. It stands to reason that, when they set up their production plants in the UK, Japanese firms bring with them their ideas of subcontractor relationship management and an intention to implement them in a potentially non-receptive, even antagonistic industrial environment. In order to understand the nature of five UK firms' experiences with their Japanese customers, it will be useful to outline the main characteristics of relationships between OEMs and suppliers in Japan.

JAPANESE OEM-SUPPLIER RELATIONSHIPS

This is a vast topic, its treatment requiring a very detailed introduction to 1) the structure of the Japanese economy, 2) a characterization of Japanese business management, and 3) the nature of alignments between firms in the overall industrial structure. For purposes of general description, we will outline a typical kind of relationship between a major manufacturer and a subcontractor. We may assume that the relationship is hierarchical: the manufacturer is the superior partner. According to his importance to the customer the supplier will be a so-called first-tier supplier (perhaps one of 150–300 firms), a second-tier supplier or a third-tier supplier. In the car industry members of the first group would be manufacturers of key components such as exhaust systems, fuel pumps or brakes. In the second group, comprising one or two thousand companies, we find suppliers of sun-roofs or moulded components such as internal door handles. The final tier comprises tens of thousands of normally very small firms offering a vast range of raw materials, fabrics and commodity components. The entire sourcing system can be described as a multilayered pyramidal network of suppliers ranked in order of preference, importance, and length of service. Note that preference may be related to the fact that a particular supplier happens to belong to the same industrial grouping (Jap. keiretsu) as the major manufacturer.

The bond between them is based on what Dore (1986) calls 'relational contracting'. This means that their dealings with each other are based on acceptance of mutual obligation: the subcontractor is obliged, come what may, to fulfil whatever is required of him to satisfy the customer; but the customer has an equal obligation to ensure that the supplier does not fail in his obligations. To explain that in simple terms, suppose an established component supplier to Honda has problems which result in defective parts or bad deliveries. Honda, although let down, 'cannot' switch suppliers. Its first obligation is to provide technical and other support to help the supplier, who in a tiny, yet important way has contributed to the Honda success story. Similarly, Honda will not abandon a close supplier when there is a slump in the market or turn to a rival supplier whose prices are lower. Such is the power of obligation: 'in Japanese eyes a relationship without reciprocal obligation is a contradiction in terms' (Holden, 1991).

With this form of obligated cooperation the supplier must aim always to meet the customer's quality levels, to keep rigidly to delivery schedules and, possibly with the aid of the customer's expertise, to strive to make the production process as cost-effective as possible. Under the three-tier system a company in the first rank may well be an exclusive supplier − so exclusive that he cannot supply his customer's rivals. Furthermore, the subcontractor management system 'generates' reliable, capable and flexible suppliers.

Single-source relational contracting suggests a very close long-established relationship between the manufacturer and the subcontractor. The subcontractor has adapted to the OEM's method of working, has invested in new equipment, production technology and new skills. By fulfilling his obligations and displaying commitment, the subcontractor is, in the eyes of the customer, a 'sincere' business partner. Sincerity in Japanese business relations always means the lesser partner complying with the wishes of the superior one, who in turn displays his sincerity by acting as a kind of protector. It is by now perhaps apparent that the general nature of these relationships makes the operation of JIT systems only fully realizable with the commitment and cooperation of both parties.

JAPANESE-UK BUYER-SUPPLIER RELATIONSHIPS

Given the radical differences in the UK and Japanese approaches to sub-contractor relationship management, it is not surprising that the methods of Japanese manufacturers in the UK have been closely scrutinized by a wide range of commentators, including the national media. In the final section of this chapter we will highlight three contributions. The first of these concerns a report compiled by JETRO in 1983; the second is a summary of the proceedings of a 1987 conference with the emblematic title: *The Japanization of British industry*; the third discusses the study by Trevor and Christie (1988), the most exhaustive examination so far on the impact of Japanese firms on UK suppliers. As well as synthesizing much of the material presented in this chapter − and in the earlier chapters too, to some extent − this short review of these contributions prepares the ground well for the case studies in Chapter 6 and the subsequent analysis of them (Chapter 7).

The JETRO study

In 1984 JETRO (the Japan External Trade Organization) produced an updated report on Japanese manufacturing companies operating in Europe. This study was essentially concerned with the future business prospects for Japanese manufacturing firms in the EC. JETRO surveyed nearly 200 manufacturers operating in four EC countries. Among other things, the report covered procurement policies and strategies, providing information on types of product sourced in the EC. The Japanese manufacturers were also asked why they might contemplate increasing their use of UK subcontractors. They had four main reasons.

First, they looked upon UK firms as a buffer to ensure stable production. Second, they could gain access to special knowledge denied to them elsewhere. Third, use of UK subcontractors would 'increase EC added value' (i.e., would help meet EC rules on local content). Fourth, local firms could do work for Japanese companies so that they (the Japanese companies) did not have to provide additional production facilities, which would involve transferring extra Japanese staff to the UK. These comments make it fairly clear that Japanese companies took a pretty instrumental view of UK firms as subcontractors: they were essentially seen as a means to open up the EC market and to mask the presence of Japanese businesses in Europe (in the early 1980s Japanese companies, having laid low several European industries in the past, were anxious to keep a low profile).

The Japanization of British industry

In September 1987 a conference with this title was organized by the University of Wales Institute of Science and Technology (UWIST). Some of the contributions directly dealt with involvements between the UK supply industry and UK-based Japanese manufacturers. We summarize the main findings.

Turnbull examined the influence of Japanese OEMs on UK OEMs' relationships with their suppliers. He noted trends to complete sub-assembly supply or component systems as opposed to discrete components, and referred to the on-going rationalization of Western OEMs' supply-base. However, no mention was made of the direct Japanese influence on UK suppliers.

Two contributions (Horn et al./Crowther and Garraham) concentrated on the impact of UK-based Japanese manufacturers in specific regions. The paper by Horn et al. compares the manufacturing performance of a range of British and US owned companies with that of broadly similar Japanese firms manufacturing in the Scottish electronics industry. Although there is considerable discussion of traditional subcontractor relationships in the region, Japanese experience with UK suppliers is only briefly mentioned. The main conclusion reached is that local UK suppliers were somewhat afraid to become too dependent on any one Japanese manufacturer.

The paper by Crowther and Garraham assesses the impact of the Nissan investment in Sunderland on the local economy and community. The paper concludes that Nissan exercises considerable control over local suppliers because of its virtual vertical integration with the UK firms and by its capacity to induce preferred subcontractors to locate on plots of adjoining land at the former Sunderland airport. The arrival of automotive component

suppliers Ikeda Hoover and Calsonic are cited as examples of this practice. Morris (see Crowther and Garraham), for his part, considers 'The who,
why and where of Japanese manufacturing investment in the UK'. This
author attempts to assess the transferability of Japanese management techniques to the EC, paying particular attention to the problems UK-based
Japanese producers encountered in sourcing components from the EC. His
main findings in this area are that the Japanese manufacturers in the UK
are wary of relying on one UK subcontractor. Therefore 'real' JIT systems
were not operating anywhere in the UK at that time.

Only one paper, that by Sako, concentrated specifically on involvements with subcontractors. In a paper entitled 'Buyer-supplier relations in
Britain: a case of Japanization?' Sako begins by outlining the traditional
methods of conducting subcontractor relationships in the UK. As for Japanization, this is presented in terms of buyer-supplier relations, with reference to the Japanese employment system. The author then highlights various
factors which inhibit the institutionalization of Japanese-style industrial buyer-
seller relationships in the UK. These factors include: 1) the continuing emphasis on price minimization in spot contracting, and 2) the structure of
British industry, with its relatively low proportion of small firms in the economy and lack of the huge interlocked industrial groupings.

The Trevor and Christie study

The most exhaustive, and quantitatively valid, survey so far undertaken is
that by Trevor and Christie. Their study, produced for the Policy Studies
Institute and titled *Manufacturers in Britain and Japan: Competitiveness
and the growth of the small firm* (1988), comprises 21 case studies: 13
examine relationships between UK suppliers and UK-based Japanese
manufacturers; the remaining eight cases focus on industrial buyer-seller
relationships in Japan. The majority of firms highlighted supply the automotive and electronics industries, and the split sample provides several opportunities for comparing Japanese and UK subcontracting relationships.
The 1988 study by Trevor and Christie followed an earlier survey by Trevor
(1985) in which he stated that the impact of Japanese industrial knowledge
on UK suppliers was a 'largely unexplored area'.

Regarding the impact of UK-based Japanese manufacturers on their UK suppliers, the Trevor and Christie study drew various conclusions. First, it was found that firms supplying Japanese customers had upgraded their product quality, delivery, and internal communication performances. These benefits tended to be associated with firms that were flexible enough to meet the demands of their Japanese customers and to learn how to work with them.

None of the contributors associated with the three studies reviewed above is much concerned with UK-Japanese subcontractor involvements as relationships. This is not surprising as this entire body of study is without any systematic framework for analysing the interactions from the point of view of relationship development. The general emphasis of the studies has been on competitiveness and the general impact of Japanese manufacturing investment on firms and regions. In the case studies which follow we shall focus on the evolution of relationships, making use of the IMP Interaction Approach to provide the conceptual guidelines for investigation and analysis. As with the export relationships, we intend to chart that asymmetrically-perceived terrain of interaction and involvement we termed 'the atmosphere landscape'.

Case studies of UK-Japanese industrial interactions: subcontractor relationships

I ask them when they will deliver the parts and they say during a certain week, but I ask them which day and what time. They reply that they cannot say. But I ask them why not? They answer because it is their way. So I ask them why not change and do it better – but they say they cannot change!

UK-based Japanese purchasing director, quoted in: Malcolm Trevor and Ian Christie, *Manufacturers and suppliers in Britain and Japan* (1988).

We are all trying to help you, but in a Japanese way. It may seem slow, and even wrong, to you, but you will be better off if you just view our way as different.

Gary Katzenstein, *Funny business: an outsider's year in Japan* (1990).

This chapter contains five studies prepared by Burgess. Each study investigates the relationship between a UK-based Japanese manufacturer and a UK supplier. Burgess's original project focused more specifically upon the impact of the UK-based Japanese manufacturer on the supplier's competitiveness. But in order to emphasize the process of relationship-building with the Japanese customer, the treatment of competitiveness factors from an engineering perspective has been correspondingly reduced. However, useful material on quality management issues has been more or less retained intact, as these are directly central to the description and analysis of the involvements.

METHODOLOGY

Personal interviews were conducted with informants from the five firms. In all but one case there were at least two informants per company. The data-gathering instrument was a question-schedule with open-ended questions. It was divided into the six sections with methodologies based largely on the IMP Interaction Approach, except in the last section: 1) the interaction environment; 2) informational exchange episodes; 3) exchange episodes relating to delivery; 4) exchange episodes relating to quality demands; 5) institutionalization of new product development; 6) overall impact of the Japanese buyer firm on the UK supplier's competitiveness.

CRITERIA FOR SELECTION OF INFORMANT COMPANIES

In selecting informant companies the following criteria were applied. The firms:
- must be presently supplying a UK-based Japanese manufacturer;
- must be first or second tier, proprietary designed component suppliers;
- must have been involved with one major Japanese customer for at least five years.

The criteria for the personnel to be interviewed were that they had considerable personal experience of involvements with the Japanese customer from either a technical or commercial point of view. Ideally the informant was also to be in a position to evaluate the impact of this involvement on the supplier firm's competitiveness. As noted above, most of the firms participating in the survey provided two or more informants, and in three of the five case studies interviews were conducted with respondents who were specialists in their function of quality, new product development or overall competitiveness.

FORMAT OF THE CASE STUDIES

The material gathered from the five informant companies has been re-presented in the following case studies to be consistent with the format of the export case studies in Chapter 3. Accordingly, the case studies comprise three parts as follows. Part A describes the background to the interaction relationship. Part B outlines the experiences of the UK suppliers in dealing with their Japanese customers. This section is further divided into 1) experiences related to quality, and 2) experiences related to technical development exchanges. Part C attempts to evaluate the impact of the investigated relationship on the supplier's competitiveness, and Part D highlights key points for handling business relationships with Japanese customers. As with the case studies about the export relationships, the names and other relevant features of the suppliers and their customers have been disguised to preserve anonymity.

Ten of their engineers swarmed over the process under test

Automotive Interiors Co. Ltd.

Our general philosophy throughout industry in Japan is that everybody is an inspector
Akio Morita, *Made in Japan* (1987).

Respondents to the question-schedule were: the manufacturing director; the senior industrial engineer; the production control/customer contact; and the operations manager/quality.

PART A BACKGROUND TO THE RELATIONSHIP

Company background

Automotive Interiors Co. Ltd. (AIC) is a medium-sized firm which operates in the insulation materials and upholstery industry sector. The company, established in the nineteenth century, operates one site in Yorkshire and one mill in central Lancashire. The 600 employee-strong mill in Lancashire primarily manufactures aesthetic and comfort-orientated goods for the interior of automobiles and agricultural machinery. The plant generates a £32m annual turnover, 97 per cent of which is accounted for in the UK.

The company possesses production capability related to insulation felt manufacture in the form of fibre process equipment and moulded interior cladding with extrusion, thermoform and assembly machinery. Although the firm predominantly manufactures goods from raw materials, increasingly it is assembling whole sections of the automobile interior. Pressure from the downstream manufacturers has precipitated this move towards supply of complete sub-assemblies, in turn generating increased turnover for the company. The use of new composite materials also presents considerable opportunities for AIC, but threatens to revolutionalize the interiors market.

AIC operates in a highly competitive industrial sector, with a number of direct competitors for each product that it manufactures. Its rivals are largely from the UK, although Europeanization of competition is increasing with the arrival of a number of German and French vendors into the UK who aim to compete for the growing volume of Japanese business.

Development of the focal relationship

AIC supplies almost all the major UK-based automotive manufacturers, maintaining particularly close links with a major UK company, upon whom it is dependent for 50 per cent of its business. The firm only supplies one manufacturer outside the UK. At present the company is supplying only one UK-based Japanese manufacturer, Sumida, a major automotive concern. Only five per cent of AIC's total output by value is absorbed by supplying Sumida. At first glance this low level of business suggests a small degree of exposure to Japanese subcontractor strategies, but this is not the case.

The process of winning Sumida's orders was a lengthy and exhaustive one, involving numerous interactions. AIC's relationship with the Japanese concern began as soon as it decided to locate a manufacturing facility in the UK in 1985. Initial talks were promptly followed by a rigorous quality survey of the AIC plant by the Japanese company's quality and production engineers. When the plant was seen to be capable of fulfilling the extremely thorough Sumida requirements, drawings were supplied to the component manufacturer to quote against. This quotation detailed the unit price cost and tooling cost for the production process.

Throughout these various initial negotiations, Sumida was represented exclusively by Japanese personnel. It was in these crucial initial phases that AIC experienced most direct personal contact with Japanese members of the customer company. Subsequently, once the relationship became stabilized, control was gradually transferred to British staff of the Japanese company.

At these crucial initial stages Sumida had reduced its potential suppliers to two appointees, and AIC was one of them. In all the preliminary discussions, the manufacturing director recalls, the Japanese were not so concerned about final product price; the vital criterion was: could AIC meet Sumida's overall technical requirements? In order to establish this, the customer's engineers – all Japanese – made thorough surveys of AIC's capability to fulfil quality requirements, production specifications and delivery schedules. Much less emphasis was placed on price until later stages of the preproduction process. The Japanese approach differed markedly from that adopted by one of AIC's major UK customers who required all the target prices to be met at all stages of the tendering process.

Once the list of suppliers had been reduced to two, the companies were played off against each other, for cost-cutting ideas and potential design improvements. Both companies were given a small prototype contract, and the aim was to effect further cost-cutting and to stimulate product development. The last stage involved preproduction runs for both of the selected supplier companies. This then led to specific requests to produce the parts, the entire process taking three to four years from initial contact. It was the policy of the Japanese company to test both suppliers' capabilities through repeated use of preproduction runs. All this was outside AIC's normal experience.

Characteristics of the exchange and organizational setting

The Sumida plant is sited approximately 150 miles from AIC's factory. All AIC deliveries are made by road, with the company running its own transport fleet of lorries and subcontracted firms being used as top-up labour.

Order-placing between the two companies takes the form of a firm schedule for the following two months. AIC's manufacturing director now accepts that there is no such thing as a contract from the Japanese manufacturer: 'all you get is a firm schedule, which may be cancelled at any time'. This schedule included the exact quantities required for each product or variation on the component. The company's production controller explained that, because of the accuracy of the Japanese forecasting, the company hardly ever had to adjust the production plan at short notice. All this showed, he said, 'the amazing control' that the Japanese engineers had over the production process. This, too, was outside AIC's experience with UK customers, who were far more prone to make, often significant, alterations to quantities very close to delivery dates. The production controller once mentioned one 'kack-handed' UK customer who sent a helicopter to pick up an urgently required batch of components. The Japanese, he said, were better organized than that.

The delivery schedule for the components required by Sumida always specified the exact time of delivery on the required day. Automotive Interiors had evolved a system with Sumida whereby two trailer loads of component deliveries were made each week. The Japanese customer made it clear that, if the lorries arrived late, then unloading could not be guaranteed and the driver and vehicle might have to stand idle for a number of hours. It mystified AIC's manufacturing director that no 'penalties' were incurred for these infringements of delivery schedules.

It was not long, however, before AIC discovered that the more predictable and stable nature of Sumida's demands made for easy production planning and that, as a consequence, lead-times were not required to be any shorter than for other manufacturers supplied. AIC quickly found that it could keep stocks at a very low level to meet the needs of its Japanese buyer; in fact its production schedulers had independently embarked upon their own policy of reducing lead-times and keeping stocks to a minimum level. Lead-times had continuously been reduced through the improvement of set-up times; set-up times for the interior cladding presses were presently as low as eight hours and setting up was done at night to avoid interfering with production. Inventory levels had also been cut over a period of time to an average stockholding of one and a half days, with a maximum of three days.

A number of factors had precipitated this policy. The fact that the finished products were bulky and voluminous prohibited large scale storage, and in any case the high added value of the products prevented this on financial grounds. These policies were well suited to Sumida's JIT (just-in-time) system, even though AIC's own system had been initiated as a result of an Anglo/US OEM's JIT system. But, in contrast to the Japanese customer, problems had been experienced with the Western OEM's JIT. The manufacturing director did not mince his words about this system: it was 'highly unpredictable, poorly planned and essentially haphazard'.

As far as AIC's production controller was concerned, there were few disadvantages concerning meeting Sumida's delivery schedules. The chief drawback was being effectively 'tied down' to a schedule which was 'not necessarily a perfect fit to our own'. Yet, as he pointed out, a considerable benefit which derived from dealing with the Japanese was the efficient, streamlined scheduling procedure. 'It forced us to take a regimented and disciplined approach to the delivery of components.'

Relationship atmosphere

The interaction relationship is marked by a high degree of dependence by Sumida upon AIC as one of its two sources of the particular exchange component. From the beginning the Japanese customer had attempted to create a close, cooperative relationship characterized by trust and openness. One sign of this was its willingness to provide AIC with technical assistance whenever this seemed necessary (see Parts B and C). In fact AIC, who had come to have virtual unblemished trust in Sumida, had every expectation of retaining and expanding their business in years to come.

Nevertheless, there had been quite severe communication problems in the early days. These did not so much stem from language difficulties, as from the UK firm's failure to grasp the basic philosophy and concepts underlying the Japanese approach to production. One of the problematical concepts was 'continuous improvement'. No one at AIC *literally* expected the continuous upgrading of quality standards demanded by the Japanese customer. In the words of the manufacturing director: 'The Japanese quality requirements were, without exception, very thorough. We've worked hard to meet these requirements at every stage: but when we reach the quality target, we find that they've moved the goal posts again. It's thorough – and thoroughly demotivating!' Now, after six years' close involvement, communication between the companies was described as 'excellent'.

In accordance with Sumida's preferences, the two companies operated a policy of minimal day-to-day communications. Nevertheless, there was frequent contact between supplier and customer for 'non-routine interactions', notably joint seminars on cost-cutting, problem-solving and new product development. The Japanese policy of minimizing routine interactions was consistent with the broader policy of embodying the supplier as an out-house production facility. The onus was firmly on AIC to tell Sumida if a certain delivery would not be met, or if a production fault occurred in a process. It was in this manner that the Japanese firm showed its confidence in the supplier.

A small but telling feature of the relationship was that, although virtually all day-to-day contact was with British staff of Sumida, AIC habitually referred to all, even locally-appointed Sumida personnel as 'the Japanese'.

PART B PERCEPTIONS AND EXPERIENCES OF TECHNICAL EXCHANGE WITH THE JAPANESE CUSTOMER

Quality and production exchange episodes

The production structure and quality attitudes of AIC had been very strongly influenced by Sumida's techniques and ideas in three respects: adoption of linear floor structures, standardization of the components design, and faster set-up times and reduced inventory. Automotive Interior's financial investment was described as 'massive for a company like ours'. But, the investment, combined with the already higher profile of quality throughout the organization, quickly brought about improvements to production efficiency and component quality.

Linear floor structure has been adopted in an attempt to create dedicated flow-lines around the factory – a nineteenth century mill – which in turn could be operated as autonomous production units. Until the arrival of Sumida, AIC had never succeeded in achieving linear flow-lines owing to the poor logistical layout of its production areas in the 'antiquated' mill. But the new linear flow-lines did their job: they reduced work-in-progress, handling costs, as well as capital tied up in materials and reworked back-logs. Strict policies of operator-ensured quality also impacted positively upon component quality, especially when quality targets were linked to earnings.

Concerning standardization of component design, the plan involved restricting the variation of components at the early stage of manufacture, so that the need to change tooling was drastically reduced. The variations in components were then designed into the components' manufacture at a much later stage of the production process, allowing all modifications to originate from only one or two core designs. Not only did this effectively eliminate the need for fast set-up times, it also allowed AIC to maintain much longer production runs, that facilitated mixed-model manufacture and flexibility for JIT.

However, the scheme was not without its critics. One of them, AIC's senior industrial engineer, commented:

> Although we do strive for continuously faster set-up times, we prefer to embark upon longer production runs. We find a quality advantage is gained by doing this which offsets the ability to undertake mixed-model production. The operator becomes increasingly experienced at using the machine the longer the batch continues, and becomes more skilled at both spotting and preventing defects. Thus faults are cut still further.

The procedure in place at AIC stemmed from an exhaustive and company-wide policy commitment to quality, which had been strongly influenced by the Japanese customer. It is not an exaggeration to say that the general atmosphere of technical excellence was the hallmark of AIC's relationship with the Japanese customer. As a result of Japanese influence AIC had instituted a quality assurance system, quality auditors, and quality circle-type groups called 'corrective action meetings' and 'senior management reviews'. Specially designated quarantine areas had been set up, with brightly coloured cages holding faulty parts. The quality auditors inspected each component and assessed whether it was useable, reworkable or scrap. Whenever serious quality problems occurred, these were promptly reported to Sumida, whose response was always 'constructive, immediate and thorough'.

Technical development exchange episodes

The habitually swift reaction of Sumida to a production fault was a key element of the atmosphere of relationship development. It also reflected Sumida's genuine desire for close technical involvement with AIC. But this was by no means confined to maintaining and improving quality levels. The Japanese customer was equally interested in joint new product development. Considerable emphasis was placed upon developing the product at the prototype stage to ensure production could be easily controlled. Following this came preproduction, a critical part of the development of a product to full scale manufacture. AIC's industrial engineer described a typical involvement:

> Ten of their engineers swarmed over the process under test, checking, measuring, calibrating everything they could. If component non-conformances occurred they suggested actions for improvement, and even a time-scale for the solutions. The policy appears to be to use preproduction runs to ensure that what is manufactured has minimum potential for defects.

PART C IMPACT ON COMPETITIVENESS

The relationship between AIC and Sumida began six years ago. At that time the main preoccupation of the Japanese customer was to subject AIC to an exhaustive examination of its technical capabilities and potential. It took the UK firm some time to grasp the full significance of the Japanese approach to subcontractor relationships. The concept of 'continuous improvement' was wholly novel and was seen as an inscrutable form of oriental goal-post moving. But, eventually, AIC learned to adapt more and more to the needs of Sumida. Not that the adaptations and the related investments it had to make were by any means minor, as the reorganization of its production layout bears out.

There is little doubt that these adaptations and investments have had a major influence on drawing AIC and Sumida very close together: AIC has become one of Sumida's leading suppliers in its product range, and Sumida has proved to be a loyal and reliable customer. The two companies have established excellent – that is, mutually responsive – communication structures and disciplined exchange procedures, especially concerning anything to do with component quality and new product development.

Over and above this, AIC's involvement with the Japanese customer has resulted in many benefits which it believes have dramatically enhanced its competitiveness. The exposure to JIT techniques, continuous improvement *and* new ideas has brought about fast set-up times, low inventory and high quality. AIC has now begun to view its production methods as a considerable source of competitive advantage over rivals. The company also discovered that it had acquired prestige in the industry as a supplier to the Japanese customer, and it attributes new orders directly to this association.

AIC also considered that the experience gained in learning to adapt to this particular Japanese customer would stand it in good stead with other Japanese car makers. It had even gone so far as to adopt the Japanese style of managing relationships with its own suppliers of machinery and parts. It had drastically reduced its own supply-base in order to concentrate on developing relationships with a much smaller group of core firms. It was working closely with these firms on developing new materials and alternative configurations. What is more, it was placing more emphasis on quality than price, believing firmly in co-dependency between buyers and suppliers, and in treating suppliers as business partners.

PART D KEY POINTS FOR HANDLING BUSINESS RELATIONSHIPS WITH JAPANESE CUSTOMERS

This case study highlights how in the beginning of the relationship Sumida, the Japanese customer, was the dominant partner. AIC was 'forced' to:

- expose the complete production system to Japanese engineers and submit to trials to prove its potential as a long-term supplier;
- adopt different work patterns;
- try to understand the 'logic' of the Japanese business approach (which was hard in the beginning);

- learn how to compete more flexibly on non-price factors.

Important learning points:

- expect to be demotivated as standards are being forced upwards to meet Japanese requirements
- wait for the Japanese shift from price factors to quality factors.

The Japanese manufacturers already here are just waiting for their Japanese suppliers to arrive

Lancsmould Ltd.

As Pierre Loti says, 'a Japanese will almost carve a flower or pattern on the inside of a keyhole on the chance that somebody might look through it'.
Richard Gordon Smith (1858 – 1918).

The respondent to the question-schedule was the manufacturing director.

PART A   BACKGROUND TO THE RELATIONSHIP

Company background

Lancsmould Ltd. is a member firm of the Lancsupp family of industrial suppliers. The group manufactures a number of household brand-names in the glazing and bathroom facilities sectors. Lancsmould itself is split between two locations (in Lancashire and Oxfordshire). At these plants the firm manufactures injection mouldings for four main markets: domestic appliances, automobile components, technotronics (technical electronics), and building supplies. The company, which has a sales turnover of £32m, employs over 400 workers, 133 of whom work in Lancashire. Virtually all of its business is in the UK.

Lancsmould possesses advanced injection moulding facilities for the production of items such as washing machine drums, computer casings and automobile bumpers in structural foam polypropylene and other engineering plastics. The firm has only UK competitors, although some European companies are beginning to move into the domestic market. German companies are seen to be emerging threats in the moulding industry as a whole. In the technotronics mouldings sector specifically, intense competition is expected from a number of Japanese moulding suppliers known to be seeking locations in the UK close to their main Japanese customers. The technotronics mouldings market is characterized by fragmentation, and is dominated by many small, low output firms.

Development of the focal relationship

Lancsmould is at present supplying three UK-based Japanese firms in the technotronics industry: Shosui, Shiozaki and Namba, all subsidiaries of major Japanese electronics corporations. The UK firm supplies components such as printer casings, typewriter bases and photocopy machine bases. These components do not affect the functioning of the finished item but they can and do add to the aesthetic appeal. The volume of business with these Japanese customers is very small, representing less than one per cent of total production. Nevertheless this business amounts to 75 per cent of Lancsmould's production of technotronics components. Lancsmould have no other active involvements with Japanese firms, but they are in the process of tendering for production of bumpers and interior mouldings for a Japanese automotive manufacturer in the UK.

Lancsmould's relationships with Namba and Shosui began in 1989; the link with Shiozaki began in 1990. The initial negotiation process was similar for all three of the technotronics firms. It began with three months of intense discussion, characterized by frequent visits by the Japanese engineers to the Lancsmould plant. Lancsmould engineers and some senior personnel made visits to the Japanese companies' facilities in the UK. There was also a ten-days' visit to some of Namba's plants in Japan.

This fairly intense period of contact, especially with Namba, heightened an atmosphere of expectation in the relationship as a whole. Lancsmould's manufacturing director was very impressed with the thoroughness of the 'preproduction communication' with Namba. For example, when Lancsmould had had difficulty manufacturing components, Namba's engineers discovered that Lanscmould's machines, one from Taiwan and the other from Japan, were unsuited to the task. The engineers not only diagnosed the problem, they also came up with a remedy. The manufacturing director was much impressed, but he and his colleagues declined to implement the remedy. 'They proposed some major rearrangements of our production and working practices. They were a low-volume customer, and we couldn't justify the investment.'

The manufacturing director also recalls: 'On all these visits in the UK and Japan the Namba people really wanted us to understand their philosophy of production and quality. We were taken round their supplier's plant as well, to get an idea of the requirements they would put on us'. At last, after 18 months, Namba placed its first full production order for three to four variants of Lanscmould's standard component of interest to the Japanese company. The contract was to cover supply for a three-year period, the estimated life-span for that component in the highly innovative technotronics industry. At that time Lancsmould described its expectations of business development with Namba as 'high'. The manufacturing director portrayed the relationship atmosphere as cooperative with a considerable degree of openness and trust. But this good atmosphere was not to last.

No sooner had the contract for the components been placed, than Namba kept emphasizing the importance of price-related factors. Quality had suddenly become a secondary issue, whereas it had always seemed to be the most important one in Namba's relationship with Lancsmould so far. Not only was there a dramatic lessening of technical (i.e., quality-related) contact, Namba merely retained a nominal sample inspection of goods delivered by Lancsmould. According to the manufacturing director, it was as if Namba was now totally satisfied that Lancsmould's quality standards could be taken for granted and was seeing how it could save money. But as we shall see, another factor began to rankle with Lancsmould about Namba's change of attitude.

Characteristics of the exchange and organizational setting

Lancsmould, which is sited relatively close to the Namba plant and Shosui plant, operates its own fleet of lorries specifically to meet the Japanese delivery requirements and minimize problems of control. But meeting Namba's and Shosui's delivery schedules has proved difficult. This, together with some lapses of service, has soured the hitherto cooperative atmosphere between the UK firm and two of its Japanese customers. It is important to understand how this situation arose.

In common with other Japanese manufacturers operating JIT systems, both Namba and Shosui provided Lancsmould with a loose estimate of future quantity requirements once a month, prior to the delivery date. But, in contrast to the automobile industry where these estimates are often very accurate, the technotronics firms tended to substantially alter quantities within a week of the specified delivery date. This behaviour was due to highly fluctuating market demand, which forced the manufacturers to revise their demands at short notice.

In order to meet this situation, Lancsmould had no choice but to keep large stocks of components in store (for anything up to three months) to smooth the peaks in demand. Under these circumstances, the company felt that there was no incentive to cut set-up times and thus reduce stocks. Simply put, the low volume of components produced for Namba and Shosui did not warrant the investment in time, engineering effort and further uneconomic delivery patterns. Both Japanese firms appeared to treat Lancsmould's behaviour as a refusal to adapt to their methods and show the necessary commitment (and Lancsmould had already turned down some earlier advice from Namba about rearranging its production procedures).

Relationship atmosphere

The relationship between Lancsmould and their principal Japanese customers, Namba and Shosui, had begun very promisingly. But Lancsmould's high expectations of both relationships have been seriously undermined. 'There is quite a lot of resentment and frustration in the company now', commented the manufacturing director, adding that he was 'personally quite despondent'. Fuelling this despondency was a strong suspicion that quite early in the relationship ('before the troubles') Namba and possibly Shosui had made the decision to place their business, in the longer term, with Japanese component firms believed to be scouring the UK for a suitable location.

PART B PERCEPTIONS AND EXPERIENCES OF TECHNICAL EXCHANGE WITH JAPANESE CUSTOMERS

Quality and production exchange episodes

Once the first full production order had been signed with Namba, Lancsmould's manufacturing director began to realize that the Japanese company now considered quality as a 'given' on the components. Until the involvement with the Japanese firms, Lancsmould's quality assurance system was based on an Anglo-American method involving front-line responsibility of the individual operatives at the machines, and worker commitment and participation. The system was supported by weekly meetings held among foremen and senior production staff to monitor the effectiveness of the system and to react to any problems that arose.

The manufacturing director believed this system delivered higher quality than those favoured by the Japanese. According to him, his Japanese customers tended to view component quality 'a bit too much like a fetish'. As he explained: 'The Japanese have a pragmatic approach to quality. If a cosmetic component supplied by us is not quite within tolerance, but it fits and looks good, then the Japanese will tend to say: "OK, it's fit for purpose". But give them a part that fits well, but looks bad, then they start getting finicky. For them the aesthetic quality must be exact.'

Lancsmould's manufacturing director had another concern about quality. As a result of his last visit to Japan he had become convinced that the quality levels required of Namba's Japanese suppliers were less than those being imposed on him by its UK subsidiary. He explained this application of 'double standards' as follows: 'Maybe their young Japanese managers sent over here are trying to make a name for themselves abroad, and build a reputation to take home. Or maybe they just think they can get away with it'.

New product development episodes

Despite the perceptible deterioration in the overall relationship between Lancsmould and Namba, communications were regarded by the UK firm as 'generally smooth'. One area of mystification concerned a Japanese reluctance to supply updated technical drawings when new product modifications had been agreed. This was in glaring contrast to the practice of European suppliers, in Lancsmould's experience. There was no knowing whether this was slack engineering practice or an example of the Japanese pragmatic approach to non-critical parts. Lancsmould's engineering staff felt let down by this lack of consideration and were at a loss to reconcile it with Japanese efficiency. The absence of information from Namba on such matters of fundamental importance tended to confirm Lancsmould in the correctness of earlier decisions about making unnecessary adaptations to suit a minor customer with a high opinion of itself.

It had been one of Lancsmould's hopes, at the outset of its involvements with Japanese customers, to take advantage of their superior R & D expertise. It foresaw distinct possibilities for joint product development with some direct involvement with Japanese R & D activities. But these hopes came to nothing. The design on final products was carried out in Japan, and imposed as the worldwide standard in the form of a duplicate part. Not only did this make it impossible for Lancsmould to make modifications on the part to design out cost, but it also made the company vulnerable to losing the contract as they were used as nothing more than an out-house manufacturing facility.

To compound the disillusionment, Lancsmould was convinced that it would only be a matter of time before one of the major Japanese suppliers to Namba and Shosui would set up a production facility in the UK and replace the domestic moulders.

The manufacturing director said that their 'imminent arrival' was his 'consuming fear'. He was convinced also that the big companies like Namba and Shosui were prepared to make 'special financial arrangements' with these smaller, specialist companies when they arrived. 'Business on a plate', he said bitterly, adding: 'The future of business for moulders in the EC and the UK with these big Japanese companies is very bad. They're just waiting for their Japanese suppliers to arrive here. Then they'll switch over to them, I'm convinced. I mean they're almost sponsoring the suppliers to come!'

PART C   THE RELATIONSHIP AND ITS IMPACT ON COMPETITIVENESS

Despite a promising beginning, Lancsmould came to the conclusion that none of its Japanese customers were really interested in developing a long-term business relationship. At best, the UK firm could expect to be nothing more than an out-house manufacturing facility. This was confirmed by the fact that none of the Japanese customers had wanted to actively involve Lancsmould with new product development.

Against that, Lancsmould had never shown any desire to make major investments in the relationship. The fact that each of the three Japanese customers was not, in revenue terms, a major customer of Lancsmould was a clear impediment, and one which probably distanced the Japanese firms – especially if the UK firm gave the impression that they could do without the 'hassle'. Lancsmould seems to have no grasp or understanding of the psychology of its Japanese customers. But in its own way it did make quite large efforts to accommodate the Japanese and their 'quality fetish'. Yet, the amount of effort required to maintain the contracts was disproportionate to the profit margins obtained. Lancsmould found that the Japanese contracts demanded constant attention for very modest financial gains. This, added to the fact that the volume of business was too small, the quality demanded too high and the price too low to fund investment, had led Lancsmould to see its future business expand without too much further involvement with Japanese customers.

Of course, Lancsmould's refusal to follow Japanese advice, though understandable in the circumstances, was a bad sign; nor were things helped by lapses of service and delivery problems. The Japanese have long memories and short patience in such matters. If several other UK suppliers were letting them down, then it is perhaps understandable that the Japanese manufacturers were trying to induce their Japanese suppliers to locate in the UK. Did Lancsmould get anything out of these interactions with Japanese customers? It got two things: first, a certain prestige in the industry for being a recognized supplier to three internationally famous Japanese companies; second, the company claimed to have gained insights for dealing with other Japanese customers, if the need were to arise. As things stand, Lancsmould will fulfil its present contracts, but is not really interested in further orders unless these are so substantial as to improve the profit margins and justify major modifications to production procedures.

PART D   KEY POINTS FOR HANDLING BUSINESS RELATIONSHIPS WITH JAPANESE CUSTOMERS

This case study demonstrates how rebuttal of advice from a Japanese on how best to meet its requirements, even if it means investment in new plant and facilities, can foreclose a relationship. Lancsmould severely failed to understand the Japanese business psychology by:

- not realizing that rejecting advice which is meant to harmonize business interests and cooperation causes loss of face to the Japanese partner
- assuming that the Japanese 'fetish' for quality was excessive and unnecessary
- assuming – without any proof – that Lancsmould would be ditched as soon as Japanese companies set up plants in the UK to supply Namba with competitive products.

Important learning points:
- any association as a (potential) supplier to a Japanese customer has immediate implications for that supplier's attitude to product quality and customer orientation
- it is fatal to assume that one's technology is superior to anything in Japan: it is a form of marketing myopia (and misplaced arrogance) that has already caused entire industries worldwide to succumb to Japanese industrial targeting.

They rely on our technology; we like that

Wigan Multi Belts Ltd.

Suppliers help firms perceive new methods and opportunities to apply new technology. Firms gain quick access to information, to new ideas and insights, and to supplier innovations. The exchange of R & D and joint problem-solving lead to faster and more efficient solutions.

Michael Porter, *The competitive advantage of nations* (1990).

The respondents to the question-schedule were: the managing director, the production manager, the quality supervisor, and the purchasing manager.

PART A   BACKGROUND TO THE RELATIONSHIP

Company background

Wigan Multi Belts Ltd. (WMB) is a firm employing over 700 people in northern England. The company, which is a subsidiary of the larger group, Parts and Components (P&C plc), produces three lines of belting products at its Wigan plant. The outlets are the domestic-appliance industry, the automotive industry and various speciality customers, such as the mining industry. Wigan Multi Belts also runs a plant producing asbestos substitute. In terms of revenue, their major customers are manufacturers of domestic electrical goods, notably washing machines.

Forty per cent of the firm's annual sales turnover is generated through overseas business. Indeed, more than half the belting that WMB produces for the domestic-appliance industry is sold outside the UK. Their facilities to manufacture automobile multi-V belts are the most advanced belting production machines in the country.

The automobile fan belt market is a fairly well established industry in so far as the main technologies for fan belt manufacture are well proven. However, the recent influx of Japanese manufacturers may challenge this existing technology with the introduction of new ideas and materials into the industry. This could precipitate a radical shake-up of the present industry equilibrium, and there are signs of this already happening in some other EC countries.

Wigan Multi Belts Ltd. faces only one direct competitor in the UK automobile fan belt market, and this rival cannot produce the more advanced fan belts. However, competition from major manufacturers in Germany and Italy is intense, and a number of French and Danish companies are also attempting to gain a stronger foothold in the UK market. This 'Europeanization' of competition in automotive fan belts is occurring as a direct result of the entry of the three main Japanese automobile firms into the UK.

Development of the focal relationship

Wigan Multi Belts Ltd. had already made contact with Sumida before the Japanese car maker had established production facilities in the UK in 1985. Naturally WMB wished to consolidate this link, especially as Sumida's investment was conditional on local content agreements. Protracted discussions took place about the possibility of WMB supplying the fan belting for the family saloon car that Sumida was planning to produce in its UK plant. Sumida required WMB to produce fan belting identical in quality and performance to that supplied by its major supplier in Japan. The negotiation over this product included an exhaustive testing procedure of WMB's 'look-alike' fan belt. The back-to-back testing was carried out in Japan by the Japanese belt manufacturer for Sumida. Once the WMB belts had passed this testing stage and were proven to be able to fulfil the product specifications, full-scale production commenced in 1988.

It had taken four years of patience and flexibility on the part of WMB to achieve this contract. Since then, however, the UK firm has produced the total fan belt requirement for the family saloon car manufactured by Sumida in the UK. The Sumida orders represent around two per cent of WMB's total revenue, but the UK firm expects to gain a bigger proportion of its Japanese customer's business with new models coming off the production line. Although there are 'non-sales advantages' to being an established supplier to Sumida, WMB needs the maximum amount of business of the low added-value content of fan belts. It is important to note that the material and technological content of this belt were quite different to the content normally employed by WMB. In turn, this affected how the firm ultimately manufactured the belts. Based on models developed by Sumida's Japanese supplier, the material was, as far as WMB was concerned, non-standard and previously had never been used by the firm.

Characteristics of the exchange and organizational setting

Wigan Multi Belts is located about 200 miles from the Sumida plant, where it makes a weekly delivery of parts using contracted road haulage firms. Orders are placed by the customer using an Electronic Data Interchange (EDI) system. Indeed, WMB was among the very first of Sumida's UK suppliers with a computer communications link. This EDI system has helped to formalize the daily informational exchanges within the interaction process. Details of Sumida's fan belt requirements are sent to WMB on a regular monthly basis in the form of a firm schedule for the coming month. This is accompanied by advance schedules for the following two months. The monthly schedule is updated to specify the exact amount of belts required each week. Experience shows that these weekly updates seldom vary much from the monthly forecast. This lack of variation between forecast and actual requirements allows WMB to keep very low stocks of the fan belts and to feel confident of being able to meet the Japanese firm's demands. WMB's confidence is enhanced by the fact that the mandrels used to make the saloon carfan belts have an inherently low set-up time. Thus stocks are not needed to cover slow tooling change-over times, as is the case in many factories. However, if WMB is unable to fulfil delivery schedule, for whatever reason, the onus is firmly on them to contact the Japanese customers and give prior notice.

Sumida's current annual demand from WMB is over 200 000 belts for the 110 000 cars it expects to produce in 1991. Even though two belts are required per car, the volume which must be produced each week to meet the demand is less than 4000 units. This volume of production is tiny in comparison to WMB's total belt output.

Relationship atmosphere

According to WMB's managing director, the communications between the two parties in the Anglo-Japanese relationship have run 'unusually smoothly' over the length of the business interaction. In the early days of the involvement, the managing director and some senior managers went to Japan to see Sumida's plant in Japan in order to study both their production methods and philosophy. They also visited Sumida's fan belt supplier. This experience of Japan, back in 1984, was especially important as Sumida was not yet operating in the UK, and some WMB managers had found their meetings with Sumida representatives hard going. The production manager at WMB recalls how difficult it was to communicate. 'It wasn't just language problems, although they were bad enough. We couldn't grasp how they actually expected us to work with them.' Once he and his colleagues had been to Japan, the communications progressed more straightforwardly. That was especially important throughout the back-to-back testing procedure in the early stages of the relationship. WMB production staff continue to visit Japan, which is seen as important both from the point of view of learning about the latest developments on production and of consolidating the relationship with Sumida.

Wigan Multi Belts's production manager summed up his experiences of dealing with Sumida as follows:

> The Japanese are no problem at all to us. We know exactly what we must make for them and for when. To be honest, their delivery requirements are much less demanding than some of our other big customers. Those firms expect you to be able to match their production needs at the drop of a hat, and from day-to-day. But the concept behind JIT is quite different from what a lot of Western firms think.

He considered that it was the ability of WMB to understand what he called 'the concept behind JIT' which had helped to promote the essentially good working atmosphere. We will return to this important point in Part C.

PART B PERCEPTIONS AND EXPERIENCES OF TECHNICAL EXCHANGES WITH THE JAPANESE CUSTOMER

Quality experiences

Sumida may like to think that it is through its efforts and hard work that WMB has been able to attain such high quality levels. However, in the early 1980s WMB had already begun a strategic drive for higher quality in response to some other multinational car makers, whose attitude to quality control had been severely shaken up by their Japanese rivals. In the opinion of the quality supervisor at WMB there was no longer much to choose between US, European and Japanese quality systems. He added knowingly: 'We wouldn't tell this to Sumida. It's vital to let the Japanese think that they are top dogs and unbeatable as far as quality is concerned'.

To meet Sumida's requirements WMB had developed a three-level quality strategy in each of its operating divisions. This was a tiered functional system which incorporated testing of incoming materials at the routine level. Patrol inspection was carried out on the next level to check operators' SPC charts. Finally, quality audits were undertaken to ensure finished product verification. The key to all of the quality measures listed was the implementation of SPC.

But, despite all WMB's precautions, once or twice there had been quality control lapses. On one occasion WMB had supplied a batch of poor quality fan belts to Sumida. The quality problem arose when a mould, which pressed the multi 'V' treads into the belts, became old and worn. This had led to a batch of belts with blurred treads being produced. The immediate response of Sumida was to send engineers to WMB who helped to diagnose and solve the problem. They identified the faulty mould and had it re-ground. The prompt and efficient action of Sumida only served to impress WMB with the highly professional approach of its Japanese customer. They were also impressed, not to say amazed, by the detailed records which Sumida made of every such incident. They also noted that 'Japanese quality inspectors positively hate dirty factories'.

Not surprisingly, WMB staff responsible for production and quality noticed quite stark differences between the Japanese approach and that associated with their UK and American customers. The production manager expressed the difference epigrammatically: 'The Japanese want to find solutions; everyone else wants to find faults'. On their regular quality inspections the Sumida people would, he said, 'treat us like partners, which of course we are'. In contrast, some of the inspectors from other multinationals were more concerned to remind WMB where they stood in the pecking order.

The production manager reported how the Japanese firm inspected the plant in a relaxed and informal manner. The visits tended to occur every twelve months or so, if the component supplies were running smoothly. He continued by commenting on the recent visit from the Japanese firm's inspectors, and compared them to the American organizations' inspectors:

> The Japanese inspectors came last week out of the blue. They were only here
> for an hour and a half, and all they criticized was the standard of our house-

keeping – which is fair enough: it's a dirty factory. But with the American quality inspectors you get the feeling they're trying to justify their own existence.
They're awkward and try to find faults in our processes where no faults exist.
It's not like they're being constructive, or trying to advise us; its more like they're
trying to teach us who's boss.

New product development exchange experiences

Since the outset of full production in 1988, communications have been
characterized by minimum interaction on a day-to-day level for routine purposes. But personal interactions are often frequent and intense when WMB
and Sumida technical personnel have to sort out production or logistical
problems, or discuss joint product development. One good example of the
latter concerns attempts to develop new fan belts and new production systems, making use of WMB's growing technological expertise and Sumida's
voluminous information on performance and acceptance by customers and
dealers. Sumida and WMB are now in their third year of new product development. As a consequence, the UK firm no longer just regards itself
as a supplier of specialist components to Sumida. In effect, Sumida and
WMB have institutionalized the relationship in order to facilitate technology transfer from the UK firm. In the words of WMB's production manager,
who relished the new dimension to the relationship: 'We're part of their
R & D set-up now. Not bad when we think that at one time they only wanted us to copy Japanese belts'.

This 'new dimension' to the relationship, quite unforeseen at the outset, drew this comment from WMB's managing director: 'They rely on our
technology: we like that. It secures our place in the relationship, and we
no longer have to look over our shoulder all the time to see who's creep-
ing up with a lower price'.

PART C   THE RELATIONSHIP AND ITS IMPACT ON COMPETITIVENESS

For Sumida the relationship with WMB was very important: as a matter
of policy they single-sourced from WMB, who in turn had persevered to

develop a close relationship with Sumida. In 1984 the involvement was one of minimal technical dependence; WMB was merely entrusted with producing replicas of the Japanese fan belt made by Sumida's long-established supplier. Eventually it has grown into full-blown technological collaboration, with a high degree of trust and commitment characterizing the relationship.

Although, as noted above, Sumida was not a financially important customer, the spin-offs for WMB were of enormous company-wide significance. Wigan Multi Belts's managing director listed the main benefits:

- the technological knowledge gained throughout the original testing process
- the appreciation of Japanese production practices and the philosophy behind them ('we rediscovered the principles of manufacturing')
- the opportunities for joint product development process with a major customer 'that really believes in R & D'
- the maximization of the R & D link to produce high-quality fanbelts for other EC countries where competition was getting fierce
- the association with Sumida was 'a great advertisement' in its own right and had led to substantial contracts from other auto multinationals
- the overall improvement in our product quality management systems, including efficient costing procedures, from which all of WMB's customers benefit.

But there were frustrations. The major one concerned the low volume of components produced for Sumida in the UK. This business by itself did not make it viable for WMB to make changes to the production structure to follow Japanese production techniques. Sumida are aware of this and indicate that any expansion of their production in the UK will ensure more business for WMB. Should the volume of business double, calls from within the company for a JIT structure would be irresistible.

Another frustration for WMB was that, because of its close association with Sumida, it had been dropped at an early stage in the tendering process for another UK-based Japanese automobile manufacturer's business. This was not entirely due to the fact that the other firm did not wish to have an association with a competitor's rival. There was a political dimension: this particular firm was being urged by Brussels not to restrict its sourcing for fan belts in the EC to the UK.

One unexpected development of the involvement with Sumida was that WMB has been applying 'Japanese-style' subcontractor relationship management with its own suppliers (with apparently the active encouragement of Sumida). Paradoxically, WMB now finds itself rationalizing its own supplier-base, 'working on' the selected few by persuading them to implement SPC (statistical process control) techniques for quality assurance.

One immediate benefit is that it now has a far more dependable supply – dependable in terms of both quality and delivery – of non-standard belting material.

PART D KEY POINTS FOR HANDLING BUSINESS RELATIONSHIPS WITH JAPANESE CUSTOMERS

This case study is a good example of how a supplier with a modest turnover with a Japanese customer can gain wider benefits from the involvement. Key points include:

- acute initial difficulties understanding Japanese requirements compounded by severe language problems
- a willingness to make radical changes to production processes for the sake of the Japanese customer.

Important learning points:

- a pre-existing commitment to quality improvement makes it easier to adjust to Japanese requirements
- a clear-cut commitment from the top of the company to the relationship with the Japanese customer is vital.

They seem to thrive on the quest for improvement

Britbat-Ueda

Improvement must never stop. It is based on the samurai tradition that a warrior (a manager) never stops perfecting his style (improving his managerial ability), and never stops polishing his sword (improving the process and the product).

N. Bodek. Preface from D. Lu (trs). *Kanban – JIT at Toyota* (1985).

The respondents to the question-schedule were: the chief production engineer and the product development manager.

PART A BACKGROUND TO THE RELATIONSHIP

Company background

British Batteries Ltd. (Britbat) is a member firm of Britpart Plc, a major UK supplier of automobile components. In 1986 Britbat formed a 50/50 joint venture with the largest Japanese battery manufacturer, Ueda Inc., by far the bigger of the two companies. The joint venture, called Britbat-Ueda, enables the Japanese partner to become a major supplier in the UK market and the British partner to take advantage of Ueda's greater resources and strong international presence in the car industry. One of the priorities of the joint venture is to exploit their joint technical and marketing expertise to expand their business in the Single European Market.

Britbat-Ueda has only one plant in the UK. This plant, in the Birmingham area, mainly produces automotive batteries for all UK-based car makers as well as for the replacement market. There is also production of a small volume of larger, stationary back-up batteries and solar cells. Independently, Ueda operates a plant in South Wales which produces specialist recombination batteries (with contained sulphuric acid) for the motorcycle industry.

The UK battery market is presently dominated by Britbat-Ueda, whose only competitors are much smaller specialist firms. The wider, much more competitive, European market is experiencing great turmoil in the wake of mergers and take-overs. The major rivals of Britbat-Ueda in Europe are the German and Italian battery-makers, who are increasingly making attempts to establish a presence in the UK market by becoming suppliers to the Japanese car manufacturers.

Development of the focal relationships

Britbat-Ueda supplies virtually all UK-based manufacturers of cars, trucks and other road vehicles. Among their Japanese customers are Sumida, an automobile maker, and Mojo, an engine manufacturer, based in the south of England and having close links with a UK automobile manufacturer. Business with these two firms, which started in 1985, now represents 12 per cent of Britbat-Ueda's annual output of two million batteries. In this case study we give equal weight to the relationships with each of the companies.

The contract with each firm is for the life of the product; and there is no re-negotiation on the original agreement. At the tendering stage of the contract the Japanese customers were 'extremely formal, extremely thorough and extremely sophisticated' in their evaluation of Britbat-Ueda as a potential future supplier. Mojo, for example, demanded detailed information on Britbat-Ueda's long-term prospects for production-cost reduction and technical expansion. Sumida, for its part, only wanted Britbat-Ueda to manufacture batteries which were in effect copies of those made by its major domestic supplier in Japan.

According to Britbat-Ueda's chief production engineer, both Japanese manufacturers had identical requirements: 'quality, delivery, price: in that order'. On the other hand, the price of the components became an increasingly important factor as the contract progressed into full production. Any price increases had to be justified to Sumida and Mojo. In the case of Mojo, it had been as good as institutionalized into the long-term interaction relationship that component unit costs would gradually fall. As the chief production engineer explained:

> The Japanese would never have given us the contract if they didn't have confidence in our ability to gradually lower our costs and continually improve. When we haven't lowered our production costs for a while, they start to take a very competitive view of the situation. Don't be fooled that they stress quality as more important than price. It's not true.

The excellent communications between Britbat-Ueda and its two Japanese customers were exemplified by the pursuit of ongoing improvement and quality problem-solving procedures. Information had been freely exchanged between the two firms during the relevant exchange episodes, and resources were effectively pooled by the parties in pursuit of a mutually stronger position within the marketplace. The process of new product development also illuminated how the firms had adopted a cooperative and co-dependent stance.

Characteristics of the exchange and organizational setting

Britbat-Ueda delivers twice a week to Sumida's plant at present, but it will be stepped up to four times weekly in the near future. The firm also delivers very small batches eleven times a week to Mojo. All deliveries are made with the firm's own fleet of lorries, and every single delivery is timed by Britbat-Ueda and the customers. The fact that Sumida and Mojo operate JIT systems means that delivery − 'practically to the second' − is a crucially important element of Britbat-Ueda's service.

The demand for Britbat-Ueda batteries from both Japanese firms is fairly stable and is based on monthly schedules supplied by the customers. As a result of the relatively high degree of certainty, Britbat-Ueda can afford to keep nominal stocks of charged batteries without feeling vulnerable to major unexpected increases in demand. This helps to nurture the positive atmosphere surrounding the interaction relationship. Furthermore, as the chief production engineer noted: 'knowing where we stand with Sumida and Mojo means that we can concentrate on other contracts and react more responsively to changes in the marketplace'. (Britbat-Ueda does, in fact, keep large stocks of uncharged batteries owing mainly to the extreme seasonality of the replacement battery market, bearing in mind of course that charged batteries are perishable and have a finite shelf life. Consequently Britbat-Ueda keep several weeks of stocks between the assembly and charging processes.)

Overall the relationships, both with Sumida and Mojo, are characterized by a high degree of interaction in problem-solving, quality management and new product development. Both Japanese firms have come to trust Britbat-Ueda and to respect its capacity for technological innovation. Furthermore, the UK firm has made major investments in equipment and reorganization of production and logistical procedures, all of which has been seen as a mark of commitment by the Japanese customers. The net effect has been to secure very close technical involvement from the two companies. Mojo, for example, helped Britbat-Ueda develop more efficient set-up times, and also helped to finance the purchase of production plant for enhancing the molten lead process control system. Currently, Britbat and Mojo engineers are trying to devise an entirely modularized manufacturing system, whereby whole sections of the machinery can be changed rapidly. 'They're behind us all the way', commented the chief production engineer.

Relationship atmosphere

Between Britbat-Ueda and its two Japanese customers there exists a positive and constructive atmosphere, enhanced through acceptance of mutual dependence, and characterized by frequent contact and communication covering all aspects of production, quality control and new product development. Crucial for the two joint venture partners was the realization that both Sumida and Mojo were far more dependent on them than vice versa. The evidence for this, said Britbat-Ueda's chief production engineer, was in the high degree of commitment which both firms demonstrated in all their dealings with Britbat-Ueda and in their studied way of using persuasion and encouragement, as opposed to 'big-customer pressure', to obtain the required levels of quality and service.

PART B   PERCEPTIONS AND EXPERIENCES OF TECHNICAL EXCHANGE WITH THE JAPANESE PARTNER

Quality and production structure

Britbat-Ueda operated all of their critical processes under the monitoring of SPC (statistical process control) techniques. These quality assurance measures had worked well to maintain defect-free batteries, acceptable to Mojo quality levels. Random quality audits by the Japanese customers had served to continuously improve the quality levels achievable. As a result, Britbat-Ueda had experienced none of the major quality problems encountered by some of the other firms in Britpart Plc who were supplying Japanese firms.

According to the chief production engineer, Japanese quality specifications were not significantly different from those desired by Western manufacturers; but there was a notable difference in approach. The Japanese, he thought, operated preventive rather than reactive regimes towards quality. This approach was especially important when small (i.e., statistically extremely rare) quality problems arose. The Japanese policy was to treat one failure in a million as seriously as one in a hundred. Britbat-Ueda production staff thought that the Japanese firms' responses to such *statistically* insignificant problems were 'out of proportion to the original worry'.

In these instances Sumida and Mojo engineers would request strict countermeasures. For example, they might insist on 100 per cent inspection for a period, or modifications to a production process or component design. But Britbat-Ueda had learnt that it was vital for the sake of the on-going relationship to treat 'every one-off quality problem as a big issue'. They realized too, that what motivated the Japanese 'obsession' with quality was not so much an idealistic quest for product perfection as a recognition that any perceived condoning of 'low' quality standards ultimately damaged their customers – the car buyers.

This attitude to defects, according to the Britbat-Ueda's product development engineer, was 'more than market-driven – it was customer-driven'. He gave as an example an instance of a customer who had complained to his Sumida dealer of acid spillage from his battery. This complaint was immediately taken up by Sumida, who painstakingly studied the battery production process to find an explanatory cause. They found it – and as a result a new battery seal was developed. Thus a potential source of customer dissatisfaction was designed out of subsequent batteries of that type.

It took the British engineers working for Britbat-Ueda some time to adjust to the Japanese approach to production and control of quality. If they felt that Mojo or Sumida engineers were 'going over the top about quality', they had no complaints about their swift response to solve problems. In addition, the fact that British engineers working for Britbat-Ueda could call upon their Japanese colleagues working for Ueda in Wales was a bonus. In fact it was generally agreed that their willingness to help their British colleagues contributed positively to the overall Britbat-Ueda relationship with their two major Japanese customers.

Sumida and Mojo did not just require consistently high quality products from Britbat-Ueda. They expected a commitment to continuous improvement whether this concerned existing products, products under development or even communication structures. This aspect of the relationship was summed up by the chief production engineer: 'The Japanese must always be getting better; product improvement plans, cost improvement plans, best practice teams. And that includes continually improving relations with us, their suppliers. They seem to thrive on the quest for improvement'.

Product development exchanges

Given the generally excellent relationships with Sumida and Mojo, it appeared to be only a matter of time before the concept of continuous improvement would reach its apotheosis in joint product development. As noted above, at the outset Sumida only required Britbat-Ueda to make batteries which were replicas of those produced by its major domestic supplier in Japan. While Sumida spent most of its energies helping Britbat-Ueda to reach the necessary quality levels, the UK firm had very limited room for introducing new ideas.

Eventually this situation changed. Britbat-Ueda now has considerable leeway in trying out new techniques for making production more efficient and for improving product performance. For example, the interiors of the batteries contain almost exclusively Britbat-Ueda technology, while the exterior remains a copy of Japanese designs. This development entailed very close technical exchange between the two firms, and, not for the first time, Britbat-Ueda had to accept the Japanese approach to specification and trials. As noted by the product development engineer: 'The specs given by the Japanese differ significantly from other manufacturers. The Japanese stress battery durability and abuse resistance as key parameters in performance. This gives us a lot of problems, as they jump on anything that might lead to customer dissatisfaction'.

As for new product testing, Britbat-Ueda found that Mojo insisted on a prototype battery being subjected to six months of tests as against the normal period of six weeks. A strict gravity-resistance test was also applied: 10G rather than the usual 3G. Indeed the battery was also tested at a temperature far higher than any experienced within the UK. It was assumed that Mojo, an internationally operating manufacturer, was really testing these batteries for every conceivable environment. But, as far as the UK was concerned, these new products were over-engineered. 'On the other hand', said the product development manager, 'that's want they want and that's what they pay for.'

PART C   THE RELATIONSHIP AND ITS IMPACT ON COMPETITIVENESS

The fact that Britbat-Ueda was an Anglo-Japanese joint venture already predisposed the company to develop especially close links with the two major Japanese car firms located in the UK. But for the British employees of Britbat, particularly for those concerned with production and related issues, the style and tempo of relationships with the Japanese customers were quite different from their experience of other UK and European car makers. Perhaps through a willingness to succeed with their Japanese joint venture colleagues, the British engineers made extra efforts to accommodate Sumida and Mojo. But a reading of the relationship development implies that all the running was made by the two Japanese firms, who were 'forced' to depend very heavily on Britbat-Ueda.

When Sumida and Mojo entered the UK as manufacturers in the mid-1980s, the UK battery market was an oligopoly, dominated by two large firms and a smaller specialist supplier. In a shake-up of the car industry, Britbat-Ueda has now gained a significant share of the UK car battery market, but has emerged as one of the two major UK suppliers. It seems impossible not to correlate this commercial success with Britbat-Ueda's close involvement with Sumida and Mojo, particularly in light of the Japanese firms' emphasis on, and unstinting support for, Britbat-Ueda's attempts to meet Japanese quality levels on the basis of continuous improvement. With many new major UK-based customers to its credit, Britbat is beginning to develop a European strategy and considers itself very well placed to secure substantial business from any other major Japanese manufacturers entering the UK or any other EC country.

PART D   KEY POINTS FOR HANDLING BUSINESS RELATIONSHIPS WITH JAPANESE CUSTOMERS

This case study shows the benefits that can accrue to the UK firm and the Japanese customer through efforts to base the relationship on personal interactions aimed at mutual problem-solving. Britbat-Ueda showed its understanding of the Japanese business psychology by:

- learning from interactions to formulate a philosophy about working with the Japanese customer
- grasping that there is no such thing as a *minor* quality problem to the Japanese
- 'forcing' the Japanese customer into a state of dependence.

Important learning points:
- The Japanese perception of quality of components is linked to a fear that the final product may cause customer dissatisfaction. It is unnatural for Japanese firms to risk their reputation by incorporating potentially faulty components from anyone. Hence, *everything* must be done to eliminate this possibility.
- As far as Japanese customers are concerned, quality is not a static attribute: it must be continually improved.

CASE STUDY 5

Quality assumes a sacred status for them

PolyACH Accessories Ltd.

There were many minor players in Japan's ascendancy as an industrial power. I think there is no question about the star player: Quality.
R.J. Schonberger, *World Class Manufacturing* (1985).

The respondents to the question-schedule were: the works manager, the quality manager, and the product development manager.

PART A   BACKGROUND TO THE RELATIONSHIP

Company background

Poly Agricultural, Construction and Horticultural Accessories – known as PolyACH – is a Midlands firm which is a member of a major agricultural products and distribution group. PolyACH manufactures and assembles complete sub-assemblies which can be bolted on compact tractors. Most of these sub-assemblies are marketed through distribution dealers, but a small number are manufactured under contract for OEMs.

The largest sector of the PolyACH's business is agricultural sub-assembly machines, such as compaction breakers and cultivators. More recently the ground-care products have witnessed rapidly growing demand, and Poly-ACH's development manager sees this sector forming an increasingly important part of the firm's business. Within the horticulture and ground-care sector, the firm manufactures turf-slitters (for the care of golf courses and local amenities), hedge and siding-trimmers (PolyACH have 68 per cent of the UK market), and ditch-diggers for compact tractors.

The firm retains market leadership in many of its product markets, especially hedge-trimmers and compact ditch-diggers, over its two main UK rivals. The agri/horticultural market sectors in the UK are currently very depressed. There was an estimated 25 per cent market decline in 1990. Fortunately, there is a global demand for the kind of products manufactured by PolyACH and the company generates a considerable global dimension. PolyACH generates 38 per cent of its turnover abroad, supplying 53 countries in 1990. The most important foreign market is France, where a sister company helps to satisfy the massive French demand for agricultural products.

Development of the focal relationship

PolyACH commenced its relationship with the Japanese manufacturer, Takemi Inc. of Nagoya, in 1985 when it was approached by its UK subsidiary, based in Oxfordshire, to design and develop a back-hoe assembly for the Japanese firm's compact tractors. This subsidiary was predominantly an assembly operation in the UK, importing almost finished compact tractors from Japan, and bolting on sub-assembly accessories at its distribution warehouse.

The Japanese firm had initially contacted PolyACH because it had been consistently dissatisfied with the quality and performance of back-hoes supplied by one of PolyACH's main competitors. By jointly developing a system with PolyACH, Takemi was attempting to design a system to match their tractor exactly and to control the quality of the product. Price and technological capability were the critical factors in early negotiation of the contract. The Japanese placed high emphasis on keeping costs down by designing the back-hoe for production. Although PolyACH development engineers also placed the emphasis of the design process on design for manufacture, ultimately the UK firm was forced to accept a lower profit margin in supplying the Japanese customer than they would expect from selling through a dealer. Problems were encountered, during these early stages of contact, in communicating with the Japanese. Even though the services of an interpreter were used, PolyACH still had difficulty comprehending Takemi's intentions fully. This was not an insuperable problem, but it certainly plagued dealings in the early stages of the involvement, especially between PolyACH's works manager and his counterpart at Takemi.

PolyACH began full-scale production of the back-hoes within a year of first contact. It supplied two models of the sub-assemblies to the Japanese firm, both specially labelled and painted in Takemi's easily-identifiable colour. For a period, PolyACH also supplied front-end loaders to Takemi, but the basis of the relationship remains the back-hoe ditch diggers.

The contract between the two firms is for low volumes of sub-assemblies, supplied at a steady, non-fluctuating level. The agri/horticultural industry is characterized by low-volume batch production of high variation products, and of PolyACH's total output, the Japanese contract constitutes only one to two per cent. The proportion of back-hoe production the Japanese contract absorbs is nearer 30 per cent.

The legal contract between the two parties forbids PolyACH to sell the back-hoes in the UK. This was a condition required by the Japanese in return for financing most of the development costs of the sub-assembly. For this reason, the back-hoes that PolyACH markets through dealers in the UK are of a different design to the Japanese back-hoes. However, PolyACH has the right to market and sell the jointly developed back-hoes overseas.

Characteristics of the exchange and organizational setting

Deliveries are generally made by PolyACH to the Oxfordshire warehouse of the Japanese firm once a month. Batches of 20 to 30 back-hoes, depending on the quantity required by the monthly bulk order, are delivered by PolyACH's own transport fleet. These monthly bulk-order schedules are estimated well in advance by Takemi, and these estimates are then updated to official orders for the following two months.

The delivered batches are placed by the Japanese tractor manufacturer into stores at its distribution and assembly warehouse. The facility is used as a buffer storage: orders are fulfilled by assembling the tractor and tool accessories from holding stocks in stores. The system does not operate on a JIT basis, and therefore the parties are not as dependent upon each other as would be firms employing JIT.

As quantities demanded are generally low and can be forecast well by the Japanese OEM, little fluctuation in requirements takes place. The Poly-ACH works manager is able to meet order quantities easily, without re-arrangement of production facilities, as lead-times from order to dispatch could comfortably meet delivery requirements. As a consequence, stocks of the back-hoe were not needed at the PolyACH plant, and Takemi had no plans to push their warehouse stock system back onto the supplier firm.

Relationship atmosphere

It was characteristic of the negotiation exchanges episodes between the two firms that Takemi always had high hopes of PolyACH being able to meet exhaustive manufacturing and design guidelines with respect to product cost. A continuous and stringent process of cost reduction had been institutionalized into the interaction relationship by the Japanese, virtually from the very beginning. In return, the firm instigated the development of a long-term relationship with PolyACH, by ensuring life of part contracts and creating an atmosphere of trust surrounding the interaction.

Takemi appeared to be acutely aware of their reliance upon PolyACH for the source sub-assembly. As will be shown later, the positive atmosphere between the two firms has been maintained by the pursuit of high quality by Takemi, and PolyACH's ability to meet these demands.

PART B PERCEPTIONS AND EXPERIENCES WITH JAPANESE CUSTOMERS

Quality related experiences

Although PolyACH had a reputation for high-quality products prior to the contract with Takemi, it had just begun formalizing its quality systems. In part, pressure to embark upon the structuring of quality practices had come from the possibility of supplying Takemi. Although the initial quality assessment made by Takemi was approved by PolyACH, the Japanese customer made no extra formal requirements upon PolyACH than any other firm. PolyACH's willingness to adopt this long-term approach to quality had improved the interaction relationship, and increased mutual expectations of the project.

PolyACH's quality manager distinguished between Japanese and Western quality demands. Where the Japanese differed, he realized, was not in the formal requirements for quality, but rather in their practical pursuit of quality. Both aesthetic and functional quality was given equal weighting, and this consideration, coupled with the demand that sub-assemblies be packed and shipped in a specified manner, had earned the Japanese customer a reputation of being 'pernickety'. In the words of the quality manager:

> The Japanese are quality-minded in everything they do. They always want best-of-order products. But sometimes this becomes obsessive, they get quite fussy, and one badly welded joint means the whole batch is rejected. On the positive side, this attitude has rubbed off on us at PolyACH. We've learnt how to think quality from the Japanese.

This attitude to quality meant that the contract with the Japanese was given 'special treatment' over many other customers. This seemed to inherently contradict the concept of the philosophy of quality. However, two distinct reasons justified the priority given to the contract. First, one reject in a batch of 30 to the Japanese meant that the whole batch would be rejected, costing time and money. Second, the parts had to be manufactured for swift assembly at Takemi's warehouse. Any variation, therefore, in dimensions of the belly-frames (the subframes which bolt the back-hoes to the tractor) slows down assembly rates and increases effort per unit. As a consequence the belly frames' dimensions were checked twice as often as those for other customers, and tolerances were redesigned much closer than would normally be required.

Once again, Takemi's obsessiveness with quality was stressed by Poly-ACH's quality manager: 'They are such sticklers for quality; quality assumes almost sacred status for them'.

Quality problems had occurred within the contract, but the Japanese firm's response to the problems had been constructive and cooperative. Indeed, it was characteristic of the day-to-day interactions between the two firms that routine communication was minimal. However, extensive exchanges took place between the production departments when a problem arose. An example cited was with respect to the slow-drying and soft coated paint which PolyACH used on their products. The paint stayed very soft throughout the assembly process, meaning the back-hoes were often delivered to the Japanese firm chipped and scratched, due to wear in assembly. Takemi's response was to encourage and cooperate with PolyACH in an on-going effort to find a new supplier of tougher, more robust paint. This small incident had the effect of creating an atmosphere of closeness around the interactions.

New product development experiences

Joint development of the second back-hoe model by PolyACH and Takemi had followed a similar pattern to development of the original back-hoe. The Japanese company approached PolyACH with the specifications it required for the product performance, such as boom-lift capacity and loader reach, and then left PolyACH to use its specialist knowledge in tractor tool accessories to fulfil the specifications.

Research on the product was carried out by PolyACH in its own laboratory, followed by prototype development and production. All this was financed by Takemi. By this process of cooperation in development, Takemi

gained a high-quality product, designed exactly to meet its own requirements and, ultimately, its own customers' needs. In return, PolyACH gained
the chance to extend its technical knowledge at little extra expense. The
UK firm was also able to develop long-term institutionalized links with a
prestigious customer by acting as an out-house expert facility.

The atmosphere of mutual dependence between the two parties was
furthered by the fact that Takemi was reliant upon PolyACH being capable of shadowing their new product development curve. In particular, Poly-
ACH were expected to be able to redesign the belly frame to fit all new
compact tractor models released by its Japanese customer. This process
of joint development helped not only in the mutual realization of the closeness of the relationship between the two parties in the long term, but it
also contributed positively to the whole interaction atmosphere. Short-term
exchange episodes related to the joint development process, such as free
informational flow, close communication and more frequent social exchanges, developed this positive atmosphere still further.

PART C   THE RELATIONSHIP AND ITS IMPACT ON COMPETITIVENESS

The impact of the total of the interaction exchange episodes on PolyACH
has been very important to the company. Although the actual volume of
business between the parties was very low, the influence that the contract
has had outweighs its commercial value. The relationship had proceeded
positively between the firms. Takemi's understanding of their dependence
on PolyACH had meant that the Japanese firm approached the relationship as potentially long term and, therefore, very important. Takemi's nur-
turing of joint product development and cooperation had generated a good
deal of mutual trust. However, Takemi were careful to ensure that their
own relationship with their customers was not harmed, and as a consequence stringent quality standards were placed upon PolyACH.

PolyACH also perceived a long-term relationship, well established and
characterized by trust and understanding. In many respects the quality of

the products supplied by PolyACH and Takemi was reflected by the excellent quality of the relationship they maintained.

Other benefits of the relationship were seen by PolyACH staff. The UK firm has been able to develop and manufacture an advanced sub-assembly model at little expense to itself. It also diversified company expertise and capability into the rapidly growing horticultural leisure-related industry and small scale accessories for compact tractors. These early links with Takemi may prove to be increasingly important in the future, if and when the customer decides to extend its own product range and the range of available accessories. This long-term perspective, overlooking the immediate decline in the market, is potentially very lucrative for PolyACH, and promises augmentation of business interactions.

Another benefit of the relationship with the Japanese OEM is the marketing kudos derived from supplying a prestigious customer with sophisticated sub-assemblies. The company is using this prestige gain, particularly in marketing the jointly developed sub-assemblies to Europe. Although initial sales of the digger were poor, more recently the product has helped PolyACH to maintain and extend its claim to be a major international supplier of a large range of agri/horticultural tools. Moreover, demand for the jointly developed product is so high in the US that the company has plans to establish a manufacturing and assembly factory/warehouse there. In Europe, the firm is presently negotiating with the German operation of Takemi, with the intention of replacing its German supplier. All of this has increased PolyACH's overseas activity in time to meet the on-going globalization of the industry.

However, drawbacks did exist in maintaining the contract with the Japanese firm that slightly soured the basically good relationship. The most serious of these problems is the fact that PolyACH were effectively disqualified from supplying new compact tractor manufacturers in the UK. This was particularly worrying to PolyACH as a number of new firms had begun assembling compact tractors in the UK. To compound this, a major customer of PolyACH had begun developing their own domestically produced compact tractor. All of this business for small scale accessories, and in particular ditch-diggers, was being kept out of PolyACH's reach – making it very difficult for the company to successfully defend its share of the market.

Another problem PolyACH encountered was the fact that they had to accept a much lower profit margin for the sub-assemblies they made for Takemi than those produced directly for a dealer. The extreme price competitiveness of their Japanese customers had considerably influenced the commercial attractiveness of the contract. Further, this price sensitivity was a continuous aspect of commercial interaction episodes, and Poly-ACH were acutely aware of not meeting these intermittent price reductions. Indeed, PolyACH's general manager felt that the firm's biggest competitors for the digger tools was Takemi's domestic supplier in Japan, even taking account of the cost of shipping parts to the UK. Although Poly-ACH's position had been partially protected by the EC local content quotas enforced upon Japanese firms, the company had still lost the contract for the front-end loader because it could be supplied more cheaply from Japan. This fact had added a dash of suspicion to the relationship.

PART D   KEY POINTS FOR HANDLING BUSINESS RELATIONSHIPS WITH JAPANESE CUSTOMERS

This case study suggests again that there are financial, technological and marketing benefits to be gained by focusing squarely on meeting the Japanese quality challenge. It also reveals that a marketing agreement signed with a Japanese customer is very likely to envisage longer-term intentions, to which the UK partner is not party. The insights of PolyACH, the UK firm, stem from a recognition that to the Japanese the quality of final products had to embrace aesthetic appeal and functional reliability. Poly-ACH met Japanese demands by:

- rejecting entire batches because of single, relatively minor, defects until desired quality levels were achieved
- permitting the Japanese customer to become involved in R & D processes – which led to joint developments financed by Takemi
- responding to Japanese suggestions on how to eliminate defects.

Important learning points:
- Never sign a joint marketing agreement with a Japanese firm without probing its longer-term strategic objectives.
- Once a Japanese customer is satisfied with its supplier's technical performance and drive to improve quality, the supplier is in a good psychological position to become a more proactive partner in the relationship.

Quality intruders from Japan

Construction of a railway [from Tokyo to Yokohama], financed in London, began in 1870. The chief engineer was English, and a hundred foreign technicians and workers were engaged to run it. Not until 1879 were trains entrusted to Japanese crews, and then only for daylight runs.
Edward Seidensticker, *Low city, high city* (1983).

The principal challenge of the Japanese manufacturing diaspora will lie in the management and organisation of factories. As that happens, it will have the general effect of shaking locals out of hidebound ways. The automobile industry is the clearest example, although the point is true of other industries, too.
Bill Emmott, *The sun also sets* (1990).

In making this analysis of the case studies in the preceding chapter, we are conscious that the sample of five companies is small for purposes of generalization and that three of the relationships involved the same Japanese company – Sumida, the major Japanese car maker. Despite this disclaimer about making generalizations, it does seem safe to say that the intense drive for quality, that shines through all the case studies, is the hallmark of all Japanese manufacturing, and there is ample evidence that, wherever in the world Japanese firms set up manufacturing facilities, would-be local subcontractors are selected and then exposed uncompromisingly to Japanese concepts of quality control.

In this sense, those portions of the case studies which relate to quality issues almost certainly have relevance for a general understanding of the Japanese approach to quality management. Thus, the kinds of issues high-lighted in the case studies may well be replicated in many hundreds of other relationships involving British suppliers and UK-based Japanese industrial customers. Furthermore, the experiences and reactions of the five inves-tigated UK firms may provide insights into how – and how not – to handle relationships with UK-based Japanese industrial customers.

In this chapter we shall consider three major aspects of the relation-ships which appear to exert a major influence on the atmosphere quality: 1) delivery; 2) quality adaptations; 3) new product development. We shall then see how these, and other factors directly related to the relationship with the Japanese customer, have abetted general supplier competitiveness. Next, there will be an attempt to synthesize the central themes that per-vade all the investigated relationships by suggesting a certain pattern of evolution that draws UK suppliers and their Japanese customers closer together. Then, in the final section, we will attempt to characterize the atmosphere landscape of the interactions, referring back to the concept of psychic distance which was explored in the analysis of the export rela-tionships.

ANALYSIS OF THE INTERACTION ENVIRONMENT

Looking at the evolution of the relationships we can characterize the interaction environment as follows. First, the Japanese companies were actively seeking UK suppliers and wished to develop them as business partners. They took a long-term view of this process, putting the potential supplier on trial in various ways. The UK supply-base did not offer to Japanese companies an immediate prospect of finding suppliers able to match the quality performance of their suppliers in Japan. We may assume then that the Japanese firms were originally very apprehensive about working with UK subcontractors, no doubt privately seeing them as both products and causes of 'the English disease'.

For their part, the UK suppliers had to adjust to a whole new pattern of work with a major customer. It became clear to them that this process might take years, and it did. They also realized that cooperating with Japanese companies as a supplier required significant investment and considerable change of attitudes. The firms that did cooperate – four out of five in our sample – discovered that the Japanese customers displayed considerable dependence on them. These same companies gained unexpected commercial and technical benefits from the involvement with their Japanese customers. For these companies at least, it may not be inappropriate to characterize the interaction environment as dynamic – involving the formation of corporate interrelationships that are unusual in the wider industrial context in which they are evolving.

One of the most striking features of all five relationships is that, for all the intensity of involvement, orders placed by the Japanese customers represent a very small proportion of the UK firms' revenue. Only in one case (Britbat-Ueda) did this exceed five per cent. On the other hand, the Japanese requirement might represent between 70 and 90 per cent of a firm's output of a given product line. All companies, except Lancsmould, expected their business with their Japanese customers to grow in years to come. Finally, we should note that though in the UK the Japanese firms must pursue their subcontractor relationships from the position of a minor customer to the supplier, in Japan, of course, they may well be the supplier's largest customer.

Delivery

Three of the highlighted companies were suppliers who were operating under JIT; one was moving towards JIT, and the fifth was not operating a JIT system with its customer, nor did it foresee its introduction. Four out of the five suppliers delivered once weekly or more – one supplier delivered eleven times a week. The fifth supplier delivered once monthly. All the companies were provided with a delivery schedule a month in advance. This schedule was updated a week before delivery. With the exception of Lancs-mould who supplied technotronics manufacturers, the UK firms found that their customers' delivery forecasts were highly reliable.

These accurate forecasts made production planning much easier once suppliers had adjusted to the Japanese requirement for frequent lower-volume deliveries. It also made it easier to use the transport fleet more efficiently, whether this was company-owned or run by a firm under contract. All the companies realized that, because delivery schedules were 'built around' JIT requirements, meeting fixed delivery times meant more than good service to Japanese customers. It was directly linked to his manufacturing systems, reducing machine set-up time, and to his quality management procedures. Thus, from the point of view of Japanese manufacturers using JIT systems, perceived and experienced delivery reliability must be regarded as a critically important element of atmosphere.

Analysis of quality adaptations

Four out of the five suppliers operated formal quality systems involving statistical control or defect-checking procedures. In all four cases these systems had been introduced before involvement with the Japanese customer. To a greater or lesser extent, the impetus for the introduction of these quality control methods had come from existing major UK customers as a result of competitive pressures from Japan.

As noted in Chapter 5 and confirmed in the case studies in Chapter 6, the Japanese customers brought with them philosophies and practices of quality management outside the normal experience of the suppliers. The fact that informants frequently referred to the Japanese preoccupation with quality as a 'fetish' or an 'obsession' underscores the difference in approach. The Japanese concern that final products should be aesthetically pleasing and without blemish also applied to components that would never be seen again once incorporated into the finished product. But a more logical explanation is that the Japanese seem to think that too many 'imperfect' parts have the effect of impairing product use and acceptance by customers.

Hence, everything possible must be done in the earlier stages to screen out defects or deficiencies in an all-embracing way. This concept of quality control works by virtue of a supplier's ability to harmonize their production and delivery with the requirements of the manufacturer. But ability in this context means a mixture of almost unquestioning compliance, and willingness (not to mention financial capacity) to effect major transformation of working procedures. Not surprisingly, as noted by Trevor and Christie (1988), the Japanese approach is predicated on a change of company-wide attitudes to quality.

The case studies make it clear, and this is also supported by the findings of Trevor and Christie (1988), that Japanese manufacturers will make very substantial efforts to help their suppliers achieve, maintain and even improve quality performance. The speed and scale of the Japanese response, sometimes seen as out of proportion to the size of the problem, was regarded as a central element of trust. The case of Lancsmould suggests that, when they perceive a supplier as being not committed to quality, Japanese manufacturers will start to stress price before quality. In the case of Lancsmould this switch of policy was also accompanied by a change in atmosphere: the previous climate of trust rapidly gave way to wariness and mistrust.

This, however, is not to say that the 'compliant' firms were uncritical of the intensity of the Japanese drive to secure the highest possible quality levels. All the informants could cite instances of the Japanese 'going over the top', where the striving for perfection seemed to be incongruous. Part of the problem, and it is a major feature of the cultural gap in the subcontractor relationships, is that the Japanese manufacturers regarded quality as a *given* and tended not always to be aware of the indirect costs imposed on their suppliers to attain the levels desired. These were costs that could not be readily passed on to the customer: hence, complaints that the Japanese business was not significantly profitable, i.e., not providing an adequate return for all the suppliers' investment in the relationship. Against that, however, when the UK firms became firmly established as quality-minded suppliers, the dependence displayed by the Japanese customer was striking.

Analysis of new product development exchanges

As the relationships evolved, it transpired that the suppliers (four out of five) provided components incorporating their own specialist expertise. Only Lancsmould produced components based virtually exclusively on the Japanese customers' designs. This situation may be seen as a function of the dependence referred to; but other factors come into play. For example, the Japanese manufacturers appear to encourage their suppliers to shadow their product development curve. Thus they gave scope to the suppliers to apply their 'unique' expertise, while consolidating their relationship with the customer.

It is very clear that the three firms with close involvements with new product development plainly relished the role of specialist R & D facility to the Japanese customer. Bearing in mind at the outset these firms were only permitted to copy Japanese products, it is striking that they had ended up by supplying the bulk of the technological content of the most recently developed components. This upgrading – to partner in technological development – not only contributed very positively to the relationship atmosphere, but also was a symbol of the evolving technological trust and dependence displayed by the Japanese customer.

Analysis of the Japanese impact on competitiveness

Four out of the five firms in our sample had very positive views about the impact of their Japanese involvements on their overall competitiveness. They reported significant improvements to their performance in relation to product quality, quality management, product technology and delivery. These are all major non-price aspects of competitiveness for which the UK supply-base had long been criticized. Of course, although these improvements derived directly from their relationships with Japanese customers, these are areas of performance which make the suppliers better equipped to satisfy new customers. As some of our informants make clear, the very fact of being an established supplier to a Japanese customer was a positive influence in securing fresh business.

Other significant benefits from the association with Japanese firms mentioned by the case study informants included: added prestige value, both in and outside the UK; encouragement to shadow the customers' product development curve and participate in joint R & D programmes; re-evaluation of company internal methods and practices; appreciation of the special demands associated with supplying Japanese customers; and upgrading of product technical content through technology transfer.

However, these benefits were accompanied by disadvantages which related almost exclusively to commercial factors, such as low profit margins on components supplied; low business volumes; perceived propensity for the Japanese customer to switch to Japanese suppliers; the disproportionate nature of Japanese quality demands; and restrictions on marketing of jointly developed products.

CENTRAL THEMES IN THE RELATIONSHIPS

In analysing the five relationships it is possible to see a distinct pattern of evolution and some common features. At the stage of relationship initiation the would-be supplier must show a willingness to conform to the quality requirements of the customer. After this the Japanese customer's quality auditors will undertake a totally exhaustive survey of the would-be supplier's production facilities. Only if the supplier appears to have the potential to meet the new quality levels will the contact be pursued. In the case of Sumida, their UK suppliers had to copy (i.e., achieve the quality/performance level of) products supplied by the domestic (Japanese) manufacturer. This stage may involve visits to Japan, both to the customer's plant and to those of relevant subcontractors. The UK supplier will then make various preproduction items which, again, will be rigorously inspected by the Japanese quality auditors. These preproduction runs are normally much longer than those required by Western manfacturers. The most important requirement is to reach the necessary standard of product and overall service quality. Price is important, but is subordinate at this stage. Considerable time may elapse before the first 'genuine' order is placed. In the case of WMB it was four years before this contract materialized.

By this time, engineering and production staff of the supplier firm may be frustrated and have doubts about the alleged supremacy of the Japanese quality systems. The Japanese customer may start to make major recommendations about improving quality. However, these recommendations extend well beyond modifications to machinery and product design. They can embrace stockholding, inventory control, cost-cutting, the entire reorganization of production procedures, quality control methods (statistical procedures, quality circles), routine and non-routine communication structures, and delivery scheduling. If the UK supplier displays commitment to introduce total quality management systems along these lines, the relationship may move to another stage.

This next stage may involve some kind of joint new product development or joint R & D activity. By this time the suppliers have long ceased to feel 'down-trodden', as they frequently do in their relationships with Western manufacturers. They are active partners in an evolving relationship with a Japanese customer, with whom they have come to identify the wisdom of 'customer-centred' quality management systems. A hallmark of the relationships is that the Japanese manufacturer is far more dependent on the UK supplier than vice versa. In revenue terms the Japanese company is actually a small customer. Throughout the entire relationship, even though the supplier may have more contact with the customer's UK staff than Japanese members, the supplier always regards the customer as Japanese.

By this stage, the UK supplier also may have gained dramatic benefits from the association with the Japanese customer. These have a direct effect on his overall competitiveness for domestic and international business development. Furthermore, some of the UK firms have been so impressed with the Japanese quality management systems that they are now trying to develop something similar with their own suppliers.

ATMOSPHERE

In the study of the export relationships we used the concept of psychic distance to analyse the interactions of five UK industrial firms with their Japanese customers and to gain an understanding of the atmosphere of those interactions. The technique employed was that of disaggregating psychic distance into three major components (cultural distance, social distance and trust/mistrust) and of treating the product in exchanges as an element of atmosphere in its own right. With respect to those relationships, it emerged that cultural distance, social distance and trust/mistrust had a considerable, if subliminal, impact on relationship development.

In the case of the subcontractor relationships the atmosphere has an altogether different 'feel'. Indeed, at first glance, it is as if the impact of cultural and social distance is marginal. In only one of the case studies (Lancsmould) has deep mistrust of the Japanese customer set in. On the other hand, the centrality of the product − as the outcome of a rigorously applied quality ethos and procedure − is of critical importance to the relationship. In this sense, this element of atmosphere has its direct correlate in the export relationships. This point will be taken up in the next chapter, when we make attempts to contrast differences between supplying Japanese industrial customers in Japan and the UK. Before exploring the influence of the product as an element of atmosphere in the subcontractor relationships, it will be useful to account for the apparently diminished significance of psychic distance in these interactions when compared to the export relationships.

First of all, in Japan the onus was on the UK suppliers to adjust or attempt to adjust to the cultural and social norms which implicitly and explicitly governed all the interactions − in other words, to conform to normal Japanese business behaviour. In the cases of the investigated companies this took much time and effort. But, owing to such factors as the Japanese ingrained sense of wariness about foreigners and anxieties about communication − or rather non-communication with them − the atmosphere landscape of interactions was not easy to characterize. Confusions over Japanese motives, and resultant mistrust, infected three of the five relationships in a marked way. Of these three, two of them (PIT and Delta) were vitually waiting for their Japanese customers to appropriate their technology, develop directly competitive products and eventually squeeze them out of the market.

Thus, 'the intruding partners' have to cope with the foreign culture and make special efforts to accommodate it in their dealings in the country of the business partner. In the case of the Japanese companies setting up their manufacturing facilities in the UK, it is they who had to consciously make the cultural adjustments. So, whereas our UK informants proved to be a very rich source of information about atmosphere and psychic distance with Japanese customers in Japan, the UK informants for the subcontractor studies were 'lacking' in this sense. Generally speaking, they did not have to adjust their normal behaviour to deal with the Japanese customers except in three important ways.

First they had to understand the significance, company-wide in its implications, of the Japanese attitude to product quality and apply what they had learnt. Second, they had to adjust to the Japanese marked preference for non-routine interactions. Third, four out of five of them had let themselves be drawn into a much closer relationship with the Japanese customers, and this was enormously time-consuming in relation to the fairly modest amounts of business placed by those firms. There was, however, virtually no recognition by these firms of the 'distance-related' adjustments which the Japanese customers had to make to develop them as suppliers. If the Japanese have big enough problems dealing with foreign businesspeople in Japan, think how more demanding it is when they must deal with them in their own country.

The subcontractors generally would be unaware that every single Japanese businessman or engineer they encountered would have had to spend hour after hour learning English both in and outside company hours;

would have had (in some, but not necessarily all cases) courses in cross-cultural communication; and would have attended seminars on their companies' business visions for the UK investment and on the thorny issue of British industrial relations. In the early and middle 1980s Japanese firms would have had the greatest anxieties about the 'English disease' (the term, in translation, had passed into Japanese cross-cultural folklore) and about using UK firms as subcontractors — firms whose concepts of quality management were, from a Japanese point of view, either inadequate or non-existent.

The strategic vision of the Japanese companies was to select and develop long-term relationships with these unpromising candidates. It is this vision which helped to transcend innate Japanese mistrust of foreign suppliers and which can be said to have become an integral part of the atmosphere of the subcontractor relationships. Very probably, the five UK firms were not conscious of this aspect of the relationship; but all were, from the outset, struck by the preparedness of the Japanese customers to think of them not just as potential suppliers, but even as long-term business partners. It was the experience of the three suppliers to Sumida (AIC, Britbat and WMB) and of PolyACH that the Japanese customers, for all their relative market power, were heavily dependent on them, not just to supply products on time and meet the quality requirements, but as partners in technological development.

Furthermore, all the informants noted the absence of the adversarial antagonisms that infected their relationships with other major customers. This, coupled with the extraordinary responsiveness to assist the subcontractors over any quality issue, seemingly no matter how insignificant, was also a major factor of subcontractor relationship development. But, everything depended on compliance with the Japanese customer. The case of Lancsmould shows, and in some ways the reasons are understandable, a reluctance to follow the Japanese way. Once it became apparent to its Japanese customers that Lancsmould was not prepared to make the investments and adaptations, the atmosphere changed. Price became the dominant preoccupation of the Japanese customers — a sure sign that Lancsmould was being 'dropped' from the strategic vision.

There is, on balance, very little doubt that from the point of view of the Japanese customers, the pivot of the relationships turned on the compliance of the UK supplier to embrace and implement Japanese concepts of quality management. The challenge to the UK suppliers was to accept the Japanese 'theory' that any compromise on quality − no matter how aesthetically or statistically insignificant from a performance point of view − was tantamount to selling the customer short. In the case of Sumida the policy to be adopted by its suppliers was 'continuous improvement', a radically different form of quality management.

Once the UK firms had displayed this commitment after the initial preproduction trials (Lancsmould failed this test), then in every instance, the Japanese customer supported its suppliers to the hilt. Where firms made major investments in new production layouts and equipment, a new phase in the relationships developed. This involved forms of joint new product development, extensive consultations on improving efficiency and cost-cutting and joint R & D activity. By this stage the UK firm had made enormous productivity gains which transcended the 'meagre' value of the Japanese business. It is illuminating that not a single UK subcontractor, not even Lancsmould with the most negative experiences, accused the Japanese of being secretive or witholding information, a repeated grumble of many of the firms marketing to Japan (Chapters 3 and 4).

PART
4

The essence of relationship development with Japanese industrial customers

The Japanese mind and its products, at their best, bear the mark of two qualities rarely, if ever, united in one civilisation: nearness to origins (Ursprünglichkeit) and aristocratic distinction (Vornehmheit) ... The blending of both gives Japanese works of art and forms of life a quality that appears not as a result of a long process of sublimation, but as a spontaneous gift of nature.

Kurt Singer, *Mirror, sword and jewel* (1989).

The flame which makes our products is in our sincerity.

From the song of the Victor Company of Japan Ltd. Quoted in: Karel van Wolferen, *The enigma of Japanese power* (1989).

There is a voluminous literature on the theme of 'how to do business in Japan', much of it produced by Japanese official organizations as well as leading corporations. At risk of over-simplification, the main theme of all these outpourings is: 'you are more likely to succeed in Japan if you understand Japanese culture'. This is acceptable as far as it goes, but an awareness of culture is inadequate without insights into the psychological world of Japanese companies and businessmen. For example, the ritual associated with the exchange of business cards (the Japanese word: meishi, literal meaning: name card) is seen as a cultural phenomenon – just another one of those curious instances of 'the way they do things in Japan'. Some books mention that the Japanese scrutinize the cards in order to gain an impression of the status and importance of 'an honourable guest'. This is indeed true, but much more can be understood by looking at the exchange process from a psychosocial point of view.

First, when involving Japanese people, card exchange is a serious process: formal and ceremonious. Executives working for major corporations will have been trained how to present, receive and study business cards. Holden (1991) reports the case of a trainee manager who had three hours' instruction during his induction course with one of Japan's major electronics corporations. To present one's business card in a casual manner and, worse, to receive the other's equally casually, is not just a breach of business etiquette; it creates an extremely unfavourable impression of the company – well-nigh fatal in a society as appearance-conscious as Japan.

When Japanese businessmen exchange cards, each seems to saying to the other: 'I recommend my company and myself to you'. After the encounter the businessmen will return to their respective offices and file the business card, even if the meeting does not appear to have been productive. (Every Japanese businessman has batteries of business-card holders.) The point is, the business card represents a *key* to the other's organization, not just the name of the contact; it symbolizes contact made and the possibility of network extension – and Japan is a business-networking society *par excellence*.

When a Japanese meets a Western businessman for the first time, the business card exchange ceremony is inevitably less stylized. It is a functional, not a symbolic act for Westerners, who are not conscious of *handling* and *transferring* their company's name. Hence there is nothing respectful in the exchange as far as they are concerned. The Japanese, if he is accustomed to dealing with Westerners, will make due allowance for this lapse. At the same time, he has an inclination to keep the business card exchange ceremony somewhat protracted. In all-Japanese encounters the exchange will be accompanied by various formulae of greeting and introduction; but for the Japanese, the English language (no matter how well they know it) cannot fulfil their requirements in this situation – the language does not contain appropriate forms.

The Japanese businessman, having said 'pleased to meet you', is very likely to apologize for his bad English. This may or may not be justified, but it delays the procedure, and he does not want to start the business discussion straightaway. First, it does not suit the non-confrontational Japanese to 'get down to brass tacks'; they like to know the person they are dealing with. Second, they need time to adjust to the foreigner's brand of English (a point all too easily overlooked by garrulous Westerners).

It is, incidentally, somewhat amusing to discover that the business card is a Western importation. According to the distinguished American scholar Edward Seidensticker (1983), the calling card, which has become 'the most ubiquitous of Japanese accessories', was introduced from Europe in 1862. No doubt the first Japanese to see the calling card in action in London or Paris saw immediate possibilities for adding more stylized ritual to all-important first encounters with strangers. In this we find something very Japanese: the adoption of a foreign artefact or idea and its modification, with improvements or adaptations, to suit Japanese whims and predilections.

This digression about business card exchanges serves to underline the approach of this book. We have not been concerned with 'dos and don'ts'; rather we have attempted to interpret Japanese business behaviour (as faithfully as possible) and let it speak for itself, but giving the reader some understanding of the influences and pressures that affect it. In this endeavour we have kept to a bare minimum the use of the Japanese words and expressions which so often infiltrate books and articles on doing business with the Japanese. The use of such terms has a way of enhancing the self-mythologizing tendencies of the Japanese, without necessarily providing insights into developing productive relationships with Japanese business partners.

The emphasis of this book has been on relationship development with Japanese customers who buy technical and industrial products as opposed to Wedgewood china, suits from Saville Row or Gucci handbags. We have not been concerned with cracking or penetrating the Japanese market or with 'how to do business in Japan' in the conventional sense. We have compared two contrasting sets of Japanese customers. But the most innovative feature of this study has been the attempt to focus on what we termed 'atmosphere landscape', using the IMP Interaction Approach for conceptual underpinning. The great value of the Interaction Approach is that it gave a framework for investigating the two contrasting types of relationship – the export relationships and the subcontractor relationships.

The task ahead in the remainder of this chapter is to synthesize issues stemming from these two sets of case studies and their analysis, in order to gain insights into the world of Japanese customers for industrial and technical products. We will begin by contrasting the atmosphere landscapes in a general way. Then we will discuss the marketing implications of the case studies in terms of requirements of relationship management, bearing in mind that the smallness of our samples limits the possibility for generalization. Inevitably, perhaps, our concluding remarks will refer to quality in the total business relationship with Japanese customers.

CONTRASTING THE ATMOSPHERE LANDSCAPES

The atmosphere surrounding the interactions of UK firms with their Japanese corporate customers in Japan contrasts sharply with that surrounding the interactions between UK firms supplying components to UK-based Japanese customers. For example, psychic distance (composed of cultural distance, social distance and trust/mistrust) was a very critical element of relationship formation in the case of firms seeking to develop their business in Japan. In fact psychic distance was, to a greater or lesser extent, a permanent feature of those interactions even when a close relationship had been established.

By contrast, psychic distance was most strongly in evidence at the commencement of the interactions involving the subcontractors. This was largely due to language problems, almost certainly intensified through Japanese anxieties about themselves as inadequate cross-cultural communicators. The Japanese firms plainly had difficulty explaining their concepts of quality management. Although language differences no doubt played a part in perpetuating confusions and uncertainties, it was as much the very novelty of the Japanese approach which baffled the UK firms – until they had been to Japan to see things for themselves. What is more, we can assume, and this point will be elaborated upon shortly, the Japanese entrants *had to trust their chosen subcontractors.*

In accounting for this 'imbalance' in psychic distance between the two types of relationship investigated, the most striking factor concerns the difference in degree of dependence between the interacting parties. One has the impression in the export relationships that the Japanese customers did not want to be – or even appear to be – dependent on the UK suppliers, at least until they were satisfied that the product supplied did not compromise any other of their business relationships. This is why we emphasized that the product was an element of atmosphere – a talisman protecting these other relationships. In the case of the subcontractor relationships, the product was also an element of atmosphere, but for different reasons and therefore its role was different, or rather was talismanic in a different way. It is extremely important to emphasize that the Japanese firms, once they had committed themselves to manufacturing investment in the UK, *had* to accept components from local suppliers. The Japanese firms then continued to work very closely with the selected suppliers in order to upgrade the latter's all-round quality performance. This process of intense technical support was a major factor in relationship development until there was, in four cases out of the five we investigated, a genuine two-way flow of technological knowledge. In the export relationships, it was not clear, in our view, to all our informants that the Japanese preoccupation with the product – its performance and characteristics – was to do with the

Japanese tendency to see the product so sharply in terms of the product's fostering of links with end-user or other customers down the supply chain. Yet, this factor emerged very clearly to the UK subcontractors – the 'fetish' product quality was obviously customer-driven.

One of the values of the studies of the subcontractor relationships, therefore, is that they throw tangential light on the corresponding and much tighter 'all-Japanese' buyer-seller relationships in Japan. In the subcontractor relationships we find a preoccupation with quality which is certainly more obsessive than in the export relationships. The reason for this may be deceptively straightforward. In Japan, if an industrial customer is let down by a foreign supplier, he is generally in a position to locate a corresponding supplier in Japan, at least for components and manufactured items. The Japanese firm operating in the UK does not have this luxury. Whereas he may be able to tempt over this or that specialist supplier (Lancsmould's great fear and assumption), there is a major constraint on rules governing local content.

This situation has the effect of making the UK-based Japanese firms especially dependent on at least some UK suppliers; very probably against their better judgement in some cases. Thus, one of the major distinctions between the two sets of relationships is that the UK-based Japanese manufacturers had no alternative but to take a long-term view of subcontractor development. But in our sample it was only Wigan Multi Belts who consciously and successfully exploited this dependence in order to expand their business with the Japanese customer. Apart from WMB the other companies in the sample revealed a certain lack of insight into this facet of business development with their Japanese customers.

In the export relationships it was only the contracts manager of Kamen, the supplier of heavy electrical equipment, who discovered that display of commitment to the customer and the intense personalization of the relationship secured the trust of the Japanese. The fact that he achieved these insights after a mere two years of dealing with his Japanese customers is, as stated earlier, a truly impressive achievement. As for the subcontractor relationships, we find only one genuine insight into the psychology of the Japanese customers. The enlightened informant was the production manager of WMB who realized that it was very important to ensure that the Japanese always had the impression that their standards of quality management were far superior to anyone else's.

Sincerity

In Chapter 4, the analysis of the export case studies contained various references to sincerity (Japanese: makoto) as an attribute that the Japanese greatly prize in their business relationships. It is important to grasp what the Japanese mean by this chameleon-like word. The essence of the term has been admirably captured by Zimmerman (1985), a particularly acute observer of Japanese business behaviour:

> The Westerner [he writes] is often puzzled by the Japanese use of the word 'sincerity', because to a Japanese sincerity is not openhearted truthfulness but a complex amalgam of ideas. The basic theme is that a 'sincere' person is one who fulfils obligations no matter what and avoids giving offense unless he intends deliberate provocation, or, put it another way, one who strives for harmony in all relationships and is always careful not to say or do anything without taking into account all the possible consequences of action.

That other noted observer, van Wolferen (1989), points out that 'having makoto compels one to force one's own thinking and emotions into line with what is expected by surrounding society rather than show one's own natural feelings'. In practice, sincerity is the quality associated with the Japanese businessman who puts the company and its needs before himself (and his family). He may compromise his conscience in the process or may become part of what van Wolferen (1989) calls 'socially decreed hypocrisy'. It is impossible to be a good organization man in Japan without being sincere, without maintaining the façade and being admired for it by others in the company. In this sense, sincerity is what might be called 'an organizational virtue' and somewhat in conflict with the Western concept. In a Western company it is possible to be a sincere person and do a bad job; in the Japanese context this would be a contradiction in terms.

In Japanese business culture, naturally enough, everyone knows what the word sincerity means: that the 'junior' business partner does everything possible to meet the demands, whims and preferences of the 'honourable customer'. It is an ideal of doing business, an article of faith, that extends well beyond the maxim 'the customer is always right'. It actually implies that the customer shall never have good cause to doubt a supplier's competence and commitment to be of service. No wonder then that the words 'sincere' and 'sincerity' are frequently used in Japanese company songs and mottos.

Sincerity, therefore, may be seen as a distinctive quality of Japanese business relationships, and it is one that is always being tested. When dealing with foreign suppliers, Japanese companies may say that they hope for a sincere relationship. They know that foreign firms cannot be 'sincere' in the Japanese way, but the word implies expectations about commitment and displays of commitment. In the export case studies, Kamen (manufacturer of heavy electrical equipment) and AngloChem, both provide vivid examples of how foreign firms can show themselves to be sincere. British Audio Systems (BAS) and Paper Industry Technologies (PIT) may well have struck their business partners in Japan as lacking sincerity.

In the subcontractor case studies, the three companies supplying the car maker Sumida – Wigan Multi Belts, Britbat-Ueda and Automotive Interiors – are good examples of sincere companies. Lancsmould, with its rather indifferent attitude to its Japanese customer, lacks sincerity. The 'not so sincere' companies, serving Japanese customers in Japan as well as the UK, would probably be thought by their Japanese customers to be lacking in 'self-respect'. This means that they have ceased to demonstrate 'prudence and watchfulness' (Benedict, 1946/84) – in other words, they are failing to keep their eye on the ball.

It is worth emphasizing that the Japanese concept of sincerity, because it has nothing to do with what Zimmerman (1985) called 'openhearted truthfulness', does not imply a party will be forthcoming with information. In the export case studies several informants suggested that their Japanese business partners were insincere (in the Western sense) because they were withholding information. The important point here is that a Japanese company can be sincere (in the Japanese sense) and still see no necessity to pass on 'irrelevant' information to a foreign supplier. This illustrates neatly the confusion surrounding the problematical term 'sincerity' in Anglo-Japanese business contacts.

RELATIONSHIP MANAGEMENT

It has been pointed out that the key factor in the marketing of industrial products concerns 'the management of relationships between suppliers and customers and the processes of interaction between them' (Turnbull and Cunningham, 1981). As we near the conclusion of this book, we propose to highlight the relationship management implications for firms supplying 1) Japanese customers in Japan, and 2) Japanese customers in the UK. In the first case we shall focus on sensitivity and commitment; in the second, on relationship-specific skills and investments, and 'dependence development'. It is, however, important to emphasize that neither of these two sets of factors is to be seen as irrelevant as far as the other category is concerned. All four factors have a role to play in relationship management with Japanese customers worldwide, but our discussion of them merely reflects their relative importance in the studies we have conducted.

Relationship management implies 'effective co-ordination of all aspects of dealing with an [overseas] client' (Turnbull and Cunningham, 1981). By now it must be abundantly clear that successful relationship management *vis-à-vis* Japanese customers needs special insights into their psychology and the socioeconomic context.

The management of export relationships: sensitivity and commitment

Sensitivity

In Japan the marketplace interaction of supply and demand does not operate in the usual Western sense. Our case studies suggest that business transactions involving Japanese customers require a special kind of sensitivity and commitment from their foreign suppliers. Sensitivity, which may be seen as a key factor in reducing psychic distance, appears to be far more important in dealings with Japanese customers in Japan than with those in the UK. This quality takes many forms and, contrary to impressions given in guides to dealing with Japan, it should be active, not passive behaviour. Sensitivity communicates itself swiftly to the Japanese, as does its opposite – what they perceive as unrefined boorishness. In Japan, sensitivity – or lack of it – is visible in one's personal style: appearance, behaviour in and outside business meetings, and voice and manner of verbal delivery.

It is worth expanding on these points for, as noted earlier (especially in the Kamen case study), the person who represents his company *vis-à-vis* Japanese business partners is a critical element in relationship development. According to the Japanese ideal, a businessman is neat, tidy, wears a sombre suit and unassuming tie. Foreign businessmen in Japan may 'deviate' from this ideal, but garish clothes and a sloppy sartorial manner may produce negative reactions from Japanese counterparts. In Japanese eyes the personal appearance of businessmen suggests a good deal about the seriousness and competence of their companies. Chapter 9 expands on some of these points.

As for personal behaviour in and outside business meetings, a useful starting-point is to accept that the Western distinction between formal and informal occasions does not readily apply in Japan. As the AngloChem informant eventually realized, it is what he called 'total involvement' with Japanese customers that counts. Being with them, whether for detailed business discussions or for pure relaxation, is all to do with relationship development and getting to know each other (however long the two parties have known each other). How one sits (no slouching, of course), how one pays attention, how patiently one answers questions or variations on the questions will all be noted – and conclusions drawn.

Quite apart from the unfettered complexities of language (touched upon in Chapter 4), the Japanese are sensitive to *style* of speaking. They can easily detect impatience and irritation. They appreciate someone who speaks slowly and clearly: not merely because they find carefully articulated English easier to understand, but because they tend to mistrust glib talk – talking for its own sake. They find it boring and boorish. The hard lesson for Westerners to learn is that they must try not to see communication so rigidly as a means of transmitting facts and concrete instances.

With the Japanese, the purpose of communication is to establish an atmosphere conducive to talking about business. For Western businessmen, learning to modulate their verbal and non-verbal communication behaviour to suit Japanese preference for evasiveness, avoidance of confrontation and maintenance of polite facades, can be very demanding. It requires a high degree of mental and emotional self-control. The acquisition of this aspect of sensitivity may takes years: far longer, it would seem, than for Japanese businessmen to understand the business dimensions of Western societies. Until a few years ago this sensitivity seemed only relevant for doing business in Japan, but it is fast becoming a vital form of marketing knowledge in the UK and EC too, as Japanese manufacturing firms create new markets for entire branches of the supply industry.

Commitment

In the export relationships it proved very difficult for three of the five firms to become genuinely committed to their Japanese customers. As we discussed in Chapter 4, mistrust of Japanese customers and their motives was a major factor. There were instances of the Japanese customers eventually acquiring their UK suppliers' technology and squeezing them out of the Japanese market. One company, it will be recalled, described its customers as 'sharks' when describing their voracity for technical information. In addition, all the companies found it very difficult to obtain information on their Japanese customer's relationships within the relevant sector of the market. Even though all 10 firms in the wider sample had been engaged in business with their Japanese customer for four to five years (and longer in several cases), this Japanese tendency to be secretive and evasive made the suppliers wary. The fact that they saw the flow of information largely in one direction watered down their commitment. The situation was further aggravated when informants considered that their requirement was not for commercially confidential information. In Chapter 4 we attempted to explain how the Japanese quite simply regard their other relationships as having nothing to do with their UK suppliers. Although this may explain the situation in cultural terms, it does little to reduce firms' suspicions of the deviousness of Japanese business partners.

The case studies suggest that one way around the problem is to display commitment through intense personalization of the relationship. This, however, places enormous demands on the individual who is, in effect, the company's relationship manager *vis-à-vis* the Japanese customer. The cases of Kamen and AngloChem showed that commitment is possible provided that an unequal balance in the information flow is tolerated. But the situation is hardly satisfactory, and it is hard to reconcile Japan's much-vaunted aspirations to be internationalized and a more open market with an established business practice such as information-withholding.

The management of subcontractor relationships

Relationship-specific skills and investments

The subcontractor relationships make it clear that becoming a supplier to a UK-based Japanese manufacturer can involve making a wide range of adaptations to the overall pattern of work and technical processes. These adaptations may entail very substantial investments in new equipment and staff development and training, and may be geared to being able to supply a customer operating a JIT (or JIT-like) system. At all stages in relationship development there is intense technical contact. Eventually this intensity is slackened, as standardized communication procedures are introduced for routine exchanges. However, non-routine matters (such as the occurrence of a seemingly minor defect) immediately invokes further bouts of intense communication.

The subcontractor case studies in Chapter 6 and the analysis in Chapter 7 described a picture different from the firms' relationships with UK and other Western OEMs. The firms that have been associated with Japanese customers for some years have, possibly unconsciously, acquired what Asanuma (1989) calls 'relationship-specific skills': skills that are specifically honed to handle the relationship with a particular customer. The case studies suggest that the skills in question are not confined to functional ones. They can also relate to a willingness to accept the Japanese way of doing things in a responsive way and can entail investments of three major resources – time, money and effort. These investments required are, however, often out of all proportion to the actual business revenue derived from the Japanese customer, but can, as we have seen, significantly contribute to competitiveness.

'Dependence development'

The cases of WMB and, to a lesser extent, PolyACH reveal a particularly interesting phenomenon. Both appreciated that they had technical expertise upon which their Japanese customers were becoming increasingly dependent. The case of WMB is all the more extraordinary because the firm had to start at the bottom of the ladder: in the beginning it had to prove itself capable of reproducing belting systems to match the quality of Sumida's supplier in Japan. Having tenaciously complied with Sumida's requirements, WMB, a relatively small company, eventually became a technological partner of the major car maker. We call the WMB strategy 'dependence development', and it suggests possibilities for new kinds of relationships between UK-based manufacturers. It goes without saying that dependence development is a very good example of cultivating relationship-specific skills combined, in the case of WMB, with very heavy investments in the relationship.

MODELLING RELATIONSHIP DEVELOPMENT WITH JAPANESE INDUSTRIAL CUSTOMERS

At first glance the two atmosphere landscapes appear sufficiently different from each other to suggest that managing relationships with Japanese industrial customers requires correspondingly different business approaches. It seems to be true that cultural sensitivity is a much more important ingredient for relationships with Japanese customers in Japan than with UK-based Japanese customers; or that coping with 'quality fetishism' is a more striking aspect of subcontractor relationships. It also seems to be the case that Japanese customers in Japan attach relatively more importance to the talismanic nature of relationships with foreign suppliers (see Chapter 4).

Despite these variances, however, it is clear to us that the two types of relationships we have investigated are, at a deeper level of analysis, characterized by an analogous pattern of development. In analysing the cases we were struck first by the fact that the key initiating factor from the Japanese customer's point of view was that the prospective supplier had the potential to fulfil the technical requirements – i.e., the UK supplier had proven technical capability. All the investigated relationships passed through phases, though not necessarily analogously sequenced, which seemed to achieve what marketers term 'closeness'. But in fact, this was closeness of a special kind; it had an unusual quality. In essence, this closeness was characterized by *dependence*.

This quality has already been highlighted specifically with regard to the subcontractor relationships. Yet a re-reading of the export relationships also shows that the ability of the UK suppliers to make the Japanese customers dependent on them was an indispensable condition of all the relationships. British Audio Systems had achieved this, showing that Japanese customers are prepared to pay for technical excellence, even if the human side of the interactions was stressful for both parties. But what seems to be generally clear is that in any kind of business involvement with Japanese customers, in Japan or elsewhere, human factors are of exceptional importance.

Thus our model of relationship development (see Fig. 8.1) with Japanese industrial customers 'begins' with technical capability and 'ends' with dependence, which is outwardly at least a technical factor. But the intervening factors are a complex amalgam of corporate and personal attitudinal characteristics, quality factors, as well as, the by now familiar, atmosphere and psychic distance. The model is a three-phase one, but each stage should be seen as an accumulation of capabilities and insights. We do not put time-scales on this model. All we do say is that there appear to be three learning phases to go through to proceed 'successfully' from *technical capability* to *dependence*. As will be explained, the first two phases are input phases; the last phase is concerned with outputs.

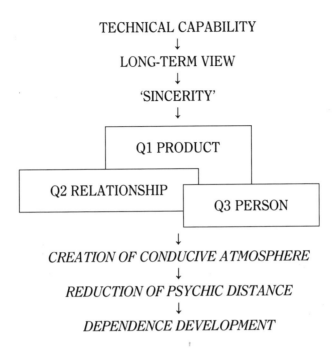

TECHNICAL CAPABILITY
↓
LONG-TERM VIEW
↓
'SINCERITY'
↓

Q1 PRODUCT

Q2 RELATIONSHIP

Q3 PERSON

↓
CREATION OF CONDUCIVE ATMOSPHERE
↓
REDUCTION OF PSYCHIC DISTANCE
↓
DEPENDENCE DEVELOPMENT

FIGURE 8.1   Model of relationship development with Japanese industrial customers

Phase one

The 'logic' of the model is as follows. In the first phase our starting-point is that a supplier of industrial goods to Japanese customers must have an acceptable level of *technical capability*. All the case studies bear this out. Furthermore, supplier firms must have the potential and the will to improve aspects of their technical capability to meet Japanese requirements. This willingness to improve, an important psychological signal to Japanese business partners, implies, and will almost certainly entail, institution of technical modifications; which in turn suggests the potential and willingness to make technical and even organizational adaptations.

However, technical capability and the willingness to improve are inadequate by themselves. These factors must also be associated with *a long-term and committed view of business development* with Japanese customers.

Here, it is not just a question of 'being patient', but of understanding that it is natural for Japanese customers to think in terms of long-term business relationships. For them the process of relationship development is one that cannot be hurried; at the same time, as part of the overall progression of the interactions, a longer-term perspective allows both parties to understand and tolerate each other more easily. Thus, as all the case studies make plain, the early phases of relationships appear, from the Japanese point of view, to involve *the testing of the relationship*. It is not just products that are under test at this stage.

The final element in this first phase concerns *sincerity* – a multi-faceted word that has received a good deal of attention in this book. Unless foreign suppliers grasp what their Japanese customers mean by sincerity – it is action as much as a state of mind – it may be that they will be, at best, perfunctory suppliers to Japanese customers on the basis of technological superiority. Business will be possible; dependence may even be achieved; but the relationship will be irksome to the Japanese customers, and a source of irritation and confusion to the foreign supplier. A relationship without 'sincerity' is one in which the Japanese partner may well drop the supplier as soon as it can secure the required technological excellence elsewhere.

Phase two

Phase two of our model is associated with an appreciation of the Japanese preoccupation with *quality* on three interlocking dimensions. The first concerns product quality and the management of quality. The second dimension refers to quality of relationship, and the third to the quality of person who represents a company and its expertise to Japanese customers. It is tempting to call these the three Qs of marketing to Japanese companies. In previous chapters we have dealt at great length with the first aspect of quality: a company-wide orientation to serve the customer through improving, and continually improving, all technical and non-technical (i.e., human) procedures. Once quality in this sense is achieved and maintained, the Japanese customer can put faith in the relationship: quality in the

relationship then becomes linked to the resulting expectations of developing new and better products, and to enhanced personal contact with the
supplier whose *sincerity* (i.e., willingness and capacity to display commitment on a sustained basis) is not in doubt.

As for the person who has responsibility for marketing to Japanese
companies, this person must be capable of personalizing the relationship
to a degree that is unusual in the Western world. As noted earlier, the
qualities needed are persistence, intelligence and tact − a set of attributes
unevenly distributed among businesspeople and hard to acquire. Though
the supplier's representative may know that in Japan the customer is God,
the path to enlightenment comes from knowing that Japanese businessmen should be treated as princes − with courteous regard at all times.

Phase three

As noted above, we are regarding phases one and two as inputs and phase
three as outputs. The first output in the last of the three phases is *atmosphere*. Unless supplier firms have the necessary technical capability and
potential, take a long-term view of business development and can actively
demonstrate sincerity (phase one); and unless they satisfy Japanese quality
needs pertaining to products, persons and relationships (phase two); phase
three may remain elusive.

All the case studies have shown the importance of *atmosphere* as an
element in relationship-building between UK firms and Japanese customers.
Atmosphere, in the sense of heightened awareness about the potentialities
of relationships, was never created alchemically; personalities were crucial.
A good atmosphere was the result of extended interactions, mutual responsiveness, a compliance on the part of UK suppliers to handle Japanese sen-
sitivities with tact and insight. Rarely was the creation of atmosphere achieved
overnight. It was the direct result of doing things right, such as keeping
promises; of understanding the boundaries of Japanese tolerance; and of
flattering their self-esteem regarding quality.

In the case of the export relationships atmosphere had two key features: 1) a willingness on the UK side to trust the Japanese partner, and

2) a recognition by the Japanese partner that interactions with the foreign supplier had not tarnished other (i.e., 'all-Japanese') business relationships. With respect to the subcontractor relationships, the paramount factor conducive to atmosphere was a demonstrated willingness to comply with Japanese wishes concerning quality management.

Either way, a good atmosphere appeared to bring about a certain convergence of minds between UK suppliers and Japanese customers: it led directly to an attenuation of *psychic distance*. This stage suggests that the potentially disruptive influence of psychological, social and cultural differences has been largely eliminated in interactions; or rather, though they may still abound, both sides actively play them down so as not to jeopardize the relationship. By now, to revert to IMP terminology, it is likely that the relationships are characterized by a high degree of inter-firm adaptations, but there is a 'twist' in interactions with Japanese customers.

This form of closeness is linked to the ability to obligate the Japanese partner to make itself *dependent* on the UK supplier. The achievement of this form of dependence was most clearly demonstrated in the subcontractor relationships, but the experiences of Kamen and AngloChem were comparable. Although on the surface the dependence appears to be technologically motivated, the case studies suggest that the 'non-technological' mechanism for creating and sustaining dependence is what AngloChem called 'total involvement'.

CONCLUSIONS AND IMPLICATIONS

Our model of relationship development with Japanese industrial customers is, of course, based on a small number of investigated interactions. We accept that the model can be further refined, and one very positive outcome of this book would be if some of the approaches and conceptual tools could be fruitfully applied by other researchers investigating UK-Japanese business relationships. One of the most important contributions of the model is that we have attempted to introduce a different vocabulary to investigate and interpret these relationships. We feel very strongly that the grand phraseology of 'penetrating' or 'cracking' the Japanese market has a way of automatically excluding several key elements from the frame of reference.

This terminological deficiency has, to a large degree, been offset by the application of concepts exploited and developed by the IMP Group (see Chapter 2). Terms such as 'atmosphere' and 'psychic distance', not to mention the general framework provided by the Interaction Model, have enabled us to gain insights into UK-Japanese inter-firm relationship development, which would have eluded us using the conventional, pseudo-military vocabulary of marketing management. But the real advantage of the IMP approach is that it sees buyer-seller interactions as forms of inter-firm relationship development. This is exactly how Japanese companies look upon business activity.

One of the major limitations of this short study has been that we have only studied the relationships from the UK side. All too conscious of this limitation, we have attempted to focus on what we believe to be major influences on Japanese relationship-building with non-Japanese business partners: anxieties about language problems and personal communication performance; the wariness of dealing with foreigners; and foreigners' putative inability to meet Japanese quality requirements.

As part and parcel of this approach, we found ourselves coming back to the word 'sincerity', that key term which crystallizes so clearly, 1) what Japanese businessmen expect from each other, and 2) the gulf between Japanese and Western approaches to business. To the Japanese their word for sincerity (makoto) suggests action, rather than a state of mind, but it is also an emotive term in Japanese business parlance. Westerners cannot approach this word through their emotions; the implications of 'sincerity' must, therefore, be grasped intellectually. Only then, or so we argue, can a Western firm develop an approach to Japanese customers that is based on sound psychological insights. For far too long it seems that Western business commentators, purporting to explain how to do business with Japanese firms, have gone 'over-the-top' about the impact of cultural differences and have failed to get inside the Japanese business mind.

In Chapter 1, it was stated that this book is about UK-Japanese inter-firm relationship development and management, and so is not a marketing book in the conventional sense. We are not concerned, therefore, to present readers with a plan for instant business success with Japanese customers. But we do hope to be of value to practitioners in the general area of marketing activity called 'the market approach' – the market-specific direction of business activities to satisfy customer requirements. Firms may produce elaborate and detailed business development plans with Japanese customers in mind, whether they are in Japan or UK-based, but these plans must take account of some highly unusual 'soft' factors: how to create a conducive atmosphere, how to coerce Japanese business partners into a state of dependence, how to be 'sincere', how to reduce psychic distance or at least understand its effects, and so forth. Such factors as these have been dominant in this book, yet they are hardly mentioned in books and articles on 'how to do business in Japan'. We hope, therefore, that practitioners reading this book will be assisted in developing what might be called 'relationship-mindedness' in their dealings with Japanese customers. We see this as one of the key prerequisites underlying a sound Anglo-Japanese business approach.

One final point. This book is unusual in that it contrasts the handling of business relationships with Japanese customers in Japan and those based in the UK. Although there is a vast amount of material on doing business in Japan, there is a dearth of systematic examinations of business development with Japanese customers in third countries, at least as far as industrial and technical products are concerned. In the case of the UK, we like to think that the publication of this book is especially relevant given the scale of Japanese industrial investment in the UK. Not only are the scale and complexity of business interactions involving UK-based Japanese manufacturers (in the major areas of cars and electronics alone) growing day by day, but also the management of relationships is becoming more critical as competition for Japanese business intensifies. The findings presented in this book should be of benefit to any UK subcontractor who realizes that doing business with Japanese customers is about achieving close inter-firm relationships, but who is mystified by the unusual nature of Anglo-Japanese business relationships.

is at the forefront of developing the relationship with Japanese customers. In the last chapter we suggested that this individual is perceived as a desirable 'quality factor' by Japanese customers; and towards the end of this chapter various attributes of an idealized 'Japan-interfacer' are listed. The choice of person to head up the Anglo-Japanese relationship is of major strategic importance, because he is the person who will be closely concerned with relationship development at the tactical level of interaction.

In the formulation of the strategic business plan for Japan, senior managers must take account of the talismanic dimension of products in exchanges, as mentioned in Chapter 3. According to this view, to the Japanese a product must give satisfaction in more than the normal marketing sense. Suppliers must be aware all the time that Japanese firms are concerned that the products of any outside organization, even a Japanese one, should not disrupt − through a delivery delay, a quality lapse or under-performance − any other business relationships. In this respect product exchanges with Japanese customers take on a mystical quality, for product exchanges are a kind of rite of passage: an initiation into a closer relationship with the Japanese customer.

So the challenge to strategic planners is to begin to see their products not only from the conventional economic and technical points of view, but also in terms of symbolic meanings to Japanese customers. This idea of the product underlies the theme of this chapter: the marketing concept, as it has evolved in the West, is actually restrictive when applied to interactions with Japan.

In the preceding chapter we described the process for relationship development in terms of non-sequential stages, from satisfying Japanese customers as to technical capability to coercing them into a state of dependence. Making use of these ideas, and taking into account our emphasis on the three quality factors (relating to product, relationship and 'relationship-handler') and the importance of atmosphere, 'sincerity' and long-term orientation, we have devised a model (Fig. 9.1) that attempts to capture the multifaceted nature of the product as the linchpin of the relationship.

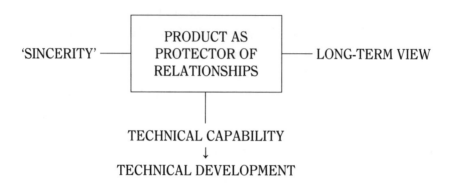

DEPENDENCE

QUALITY OF RELATIONSHIP

QUALITY OF INTERFACER

QUALITY OF PRODUCT

'SINCERITY' — | PRODUCT AS PROTECTOR OF RELATIONSHIPS | — LONG-TERM VIEW

TECHNICAL CAPABILITY
↓
TECHNICAL DEVELOPMENT

POSITIVE ATMOSPHERE

FIGURE 9.1   Model showing the product as the linchpin of relationship building with Japanese customers

What we wish to emphasize with this model is the conviction that, to the Japanese customer, the supplier's product represents not only a technical and economic worth, but also symbolic values about how the Japanese like to do business.

Specifying of tactics

In the above section it was suggested that firms must grip their Japanese customers into relationships. This strategic requirement must be underpinned by a consciously tactical orientation to relationship management and business development. Such an orientation is necessary precisely because – and this point is never given enough prominence – the Japanese are master-tacticians in the game of business.

The Western management preoccupation with Japanese business strategy has, in our view, led to *an underestimation of Japanese tactical behaviour,* both in all-Japanese business relationships as well as in relationships involving the Japanese with non-Japanese. Therefore as it comes second nature to the Japanese to think and act tactically in all their business relationships, it is extremely important that their actual and would-be suppliers understand what is involved and why their own response should be tactically planned.

The key tactical position for a UK firm to adopt is one which contributes positively to a good working atmosphere. The most important element of atmosphere, from a Japanese perspective, is good previous experiences, i.e., the foreign supplier has proved to be 'sincere' and has lived up to promises and not created problems for the Japanese customer with the latter's other business relationships. In other words, to hark back to the beginning of this chapter, the supplier has *anticipated* well.

The next most important element is the 'Japan-interfacer', of whom more will be said in a later section. But here we can mention that there are four key ways in which the interfacer contributes to atmosphere. First is the general impression of personality and character; second is overall job competence; third is the capacity to handle the Japanese, their foibles and often exasperating punctiliousness; fourth is skill in speaking English patiently and comprehensibly, bearing in mind the complexity of personal communication with Japanese counterparts.

Relationship review as monitoring

Writers on strategic management emphasize, rightly, that it is of vital importance to monitor and test the efficiency of the strategic plan as it evolves. Monitoring, which is of course essential for corrective action, depends on feedback. But, when dealing with Japanese customers, this is a problem: clear-cut feedback is often simply not forthcoming.

Our case studies show that the absence or vague dispensing of feedback was a major irritant in relationships, and a major source of distrust and antagonism. However, two case studies – Kamen and Anglochem –

showed that a tactful disregard of the need for direct feedback appeared to ensure that the relationships flourished. The subcontractor relationships, which focused very strongly on technical features, demonstrated that those firms which had proven themselves technically invariably found considerable responsiveness from the Japanese customer. In this sense, again, conventional ideas of monitoring appear to be both limited and inappropriate.

The case studies show that Japanese customers lay great store by particular demonstrations of responsiveness, both to the market conditions in which they are operating and to the Japanese companies' own demands. Many of these demands can strike some suppliers as idiosyncratic and superfluous. Therefore an important part of monitoring business development with Japanese customers should specifically involve *relationship review*. Indeed we would go so far as to say that a monitoring programme for Japanese customers that does *not* make relationship review its central element is ill-conceived from the outset.

The starting point for undertaking the relationship review is an understanding of the nature of, and logic behind, Japanese aspirations as customers and the kinds of demand they make on their suppliers. To make things plain, we shall list various categories of Japanese demands and then show what we believe to be successful, i.e., psychologically appropriate, responses. The various demands and responses listed below have all emanated from our case studies, and they relate to the following issues which a worthwhile relationship review must incorporate: quality demands; product demands; relationship commitment; communication; and relationship atmosphere.

Demand: quality
Japanese demands on quality are characterized by an insistence on process and product quality factors extending beyond normal cost-benefit considerations.

Appropriate responses entail:
1 Being prepared, initially, to try to understand or at least accept Japanese 'logic' in order to show commitment.

2 Carrying out changes to quality procedures as requested.
3 Accepting that changes involve continuous trials and that it may take some years to become an approved supplier.
4 Being prepared to absorb the economic cost of these requirements, but bearing in mind that there can be long-term benefits to the supplier in terms of overall product quality gained and even new markets.

Demand: product

Here the challenge to the supplier is to grasp that the product has symbolic meanings for Japanese customers which extend beyond the 'normal' functional, economic and aesthetic dimensions.

The appropriate responses entail:
1 Appreciating the link in the Japanese mind between the desire to achieve the highest quality feasible for the protection of other business relationships.

Demand: relationship commitment

The Japanese aspire to have long-term relationships.

The appropriate responses are based on the recognition that:
1 the Japanese appear to have a psychological need for long-term relationships.
2 this need must be met by establishing a long-term time-scale in the company's strategic plan.
3 strong top-management support is needed for the company's designated Japan-interfacer, who may have to devote many years to this involvement with Japan and Japanese business.
4 the Japanese do not have a static view of relationships – they are mutable and dynamic.

Demand: communication

The Japanese suffer from 'communication malaise' (see Chapter 4), a complicated condition involving language issues, mutual perceptions (or rather misperceptions), and the Japanese world-view.

The appropriate response entails:
1 Accepting that the Japanese are not always capable of sending clear messages to Westerners, but that behind this lies the (occasionally rather piteous) 'please-try-to-understand-us' syndrome.
2 Demonstrating, articulating and enacting a continuous willingness to try to understand them, to see things from their admittedly often unusual perspective. Making modifications to processes and products especially for the Japanese customer (and letting him know so) is such an enactment.

Demand: atmosphere
To the Japanese a business relationship cannot proceed unless the atmosphere is right: that complex amalgam of positive past experiences, shared mutuality of understanding and long-term purpose, and good human relationships binding supplier and customer.

The appropriate responses recognize:
1 Atmosphere is a live and vital element of business relationships to Japan customers. The supplier must conscientiously contribute to atmosphere at the corporate and personal levels of interaction.
2 The application of intelligence, courtesy and tact in all interactions with Japanese customers is vital.
3 The relationship must be fronted by a company representative who is willing and able to commit himself to total involvement in the pursuit of relationship development with Japanese customers.

The point to grasp about this concept of monitoring relationship development is that it represents a mechanism for understanding Japanese customers and their behaviour, as feedback from them may be variously misleading, vague or non-existent.

In this chapter, and on several occasions in this book, we have stressed the importance of the qualities and competence of the person we have termed 'the Japan-interfacer'. This is the person with the key task of communicating business objectives and developing relationships in ways that are compatible with the Japanese world-view, including their preferences for how interactions with non-Japanese business partners ought to proceed. In the next section of this book we turn our attention to the Japan-interfacer.

THE JAPAN-INTERFACER

Firms must grasp that the choice of individual who represents them *vis-à-vis* their Japanese customers has strategic influence over relationship development and the productiveness of business interactions. Their functional specialists, who may be experienced in dealing with 'aggressive' customers in countries such as Germany or the USA, may not have the blend of job competencies that are best suited to handling relationships with Japanese customers. To hark back to the importance of infusing intelligence and tact into UK-Japanese business interactions, the deficient element may often be tact rather than intelligence (though that helps).

The case studies, particularly those examining the export relationships, made it crystal-clear that the more successful firms were those in which the Japan interfacer personified company commitment and competence. A specific feature of the commitment was a willingness on the part of the individuals to devote a substantial amount of their career to the involvement with their Japanese customers. Firms with a strong interest in doing business with Japanese firms, but who do not have a person able to fulfil this role are at a certain strategic disadvantage: the Japanese customer is deprived of someone they can trust both to sort out short-term problems and develop the longer-term relationship. Again, the case studies endorsed this point of view.

All the evidence surveyed in this book suggests that the individual manager with responsibilities for business with Japanese customers needs a complex set of personal and professional attributes. It is, of course, hard to imagine any one person embodying all these attributes, which are presented below as pointers rather than absolute characteristics. Rather than produce a list of random factors, the attributes are classified as follows: personal behaviour and attitudes; communication behaviour; Japan orientation; and business orientation.

Personal behaviour and attitudes

An effective Japan-interfacer should:

- not be prone to outbursts of vexation or irritation
- be politely persistent and *always* mask impatience
- know how to dissemble (yes, dissemble!)
- be personally unassuming and not be bombastic
- be willing to see beyond the stereotypes
- apply intelligence and tact to all interactions with Japanese people.

Communication behaviour

The Japan-interfacer should:

- speak and write grammatically correct English
- not be given to speaking loudly or interrupting
- know when to drop a topic or even when to say nothing
- learn how to use small talk in creating a good impression
- appreciate the importance of thanking and apologizing
- learn something about the Japanese language and its role in Japanese society.

Japan orientation

The Japan-interfacer will know that a successful Japan orientation entails:

- respecting Japanese technological talent
- not underestimating the Japanese capacity for the organization and implementation of complex projects
- accepting that behind every Japanese requirement, no matter how trivial or unnecessary it may appear, there is an important need to be satisfied
- being mindful of behaving as befits a foreigner in Japanese eyes
- reading a good deal about Japan
- striving to create a good atmosphere
- striving to make a good impression
- dealing with the Japanese respectfully.

Business orientation

In their business orientation, Japan-interfacers are at an advantage if they:

- have international experience and outlook
- know that they symbolize their firms' capability and commitment
- are always striving to create exchange opportunities
- see relationship-building as central to business development.

In a nutshell, the Japan-interfacer *actively reduces the degree of psychic distance in relationships and gets the Japanese to trust him*. As an afterthought concerning communication behaviour, it is no by means easy to explain precisely how Japan-interfacers of every description should modify their English in anticipation of Japanese language and communication difficulties. However, a useful attribute is sufficient knowledge of *any* foreign language to appreciate that language barriers are not just a function of foreigners' imperfect comprehension of *your* English, but also a result of your own blindness to your relative unintelligibility to non-native speakers of English.

CONCLUSION

The theme of this chapter is that the marketing concept, although it stresses the central importance of customers and the satisfaction of their needs, is not sufficiently robust to embrace the requirements of Japanese customers who have needs that extend beyond the 'normal' ones. Take the idea of the product, for example. We argue that for Japanese customers products must be seen in what we called talismanic terms: they must protect customers' other relationships in a slightly mystical way that 'hard-nosed' marketers from the West may find quaint or naive. We have argued that the term 'quality' should not just apply to products, but also to 1) the Japan-interfacer in terms of personality, disposition and professional competence, and 2) the actual character of the business relationship.

We stressed that Japanese firms appear to need long-term relationships. This kind of need has not, as far as we can tell, been identified as a need that marketing people should actively seek to understand and address. We further identified atmosphere as a key element of relationships, and products as an element of atmosphere. Thus it seems to us that we need some kind of modified marketing concept for Japanese customers. We believe that the key to creating this modified marketing concept lies in 1) understanding the Japanese need for long-term relationships, which is not a particularly difficult notion to take on board, and 2) accepting the idea that the product in exchange processes is an element of atmosphere and not just a vehicle for satisfying customer needs in the conventional way.

Understanding the product from this, admittedly unusual, perspective is central to appreciating the crucially important psychological dimension of handling business relationships with Japanese customers in Japan or elsewhere.

References and further reading

Abbeglen, J.C. and Stalk, G. (1985). *Kaisha: The Japanese corporation.* New York: Basic Books

Abrahamsen, M. (1992). 'The extent and impact of psychic distance on long-term business relationships between British suppliers and Japanese customers in industrial markets'. Unpublished MSc thesis, University of Manchester Institute of Science and Technology

Anglo-Japanese Journal (1991). 'Japan and the regeneration of British industry', London: Anglo-Japanese Economic Institute, Vol. 4, No. 4, May–August 1991

Anglo-Japanese Journal (1991). 'Japanese cars make their marque in Britain', London: Anglo-Japanese Economic Institute, Vol. 4, No. 4, Jan–March

Artzt, E. (1989). 'Winning in Japan: Keys to global success'. *Business Quarterly,* Vol. 5, No. 3

Asanuma, B. (1989). 'Manufacturer-supplier relationships in Japan and the concept of relationship-specific skill', *Journal of Japanese and International Economics,* Vol. 3

Beckerman, W. (1956). 'Distance and the pattern of intra-European trade', *Review of Economics and Statistics, Vol. 38*

Benedict, R. (1984; first published in 1946). *The chrysanthemum and the sword.* Tokyo: Charles E. Tuttle

Best, W.J. (1990). 'Western companies in Japan: relearning the basics', *Directors and Boards,* Vol. 14, No. 4

Boxer, C.R. (1974). *The Christian century in Japan.* Berkeley: University of California Press

Burgess, M. (1991). 'The impact of UK-based Japanese manufacturers on UK supplier's competitiveness'. Unpublished MEng Dissertation, Department of Mechanical Engineering, UMIST, Manchester

Buruma, I. (1988). *A Japanese mirror: Heroes and villains of Japanese culture.* London: Penguin Books

Carr, C. (1990). *Britain's competitiveness: The management of the vehicle component industry.* London: Routledge

Chamberlain, B.H. (1982; first published in 1904). *Japanese things: Being notes on various subjects connected with Japan.* Tokyo: Charles E. Tuttle

Chisnall, P.M. (1981). *Marketing research: Analysis and measurement.* London: McGraw-Hill

Chisnall, P.M. (1984). *Marketing: a behavioural approach.* London: McGraw-Hill

Christopher, R. (1984). *The Japanese mind.* London: Pan Books

Cooper, M. (ed). (1981). *They came to Japan: An anthology of European reports on Japan, 1543–1640.* Berkeley: University of California Press

Crowther, S. and Garraham, P. (1987). Invitation to Sunderland: Corporate power and local economy. Unpublished paper to the UWIST conference on the Japanization of British industry

Cunningham, M.T. and Homse, E. (1986). 'Controlling the marketing-purchasing interface: Resource development and organisational implications'. *Industrial Marketing and Purchasing*, Vol. 1, No. 2

Dale, P. (1990). *The myth of Japanese uniqueness*. London: Routledge

Dambmann, G. (1986). *Japan: Weltmacht als Einzelgaenger*. Munich: Piper Verlag

Department of Trade and Industry, 1988. *Competitive manufacturing: A practical approach to the development of manufacturing strategy*. London: DTI

Dillon, L.S. (1990). 'The occidental tourist'. *Training & Development Journal*, Vol. 44, No. 5

Dore, R. (1986). *Flexible rigidities: Industrial policy and structural readjustment in the Japanese economy 1970-1980*. London: The Athlone Press

Dower, J. (1986). *War without mercy: Race and power in the Pacific War*. London: Faber and Faber

Drucker, P. (1973). *Management: Tasks, responsibilities, practices*. New York: Harper & Row

Economist, 1991. 'Edith the First', 18 May

Elmashmawi, F. (1990). 'Japanese culture clash in multicultural management'. *Tokyo Business Today*, Vol. 58, No. 2

Emmott, B. (1990). *The sun also sets: Why Japan will not be number one*. London: Simon & Schuster

Engineer, (1989). 'Coming to terms with the times', 31 August

Engineer, (1990). 'The Good European', 5 July

Finneston, M. (Chairman) (1980). *Royal Commission of Enquiry into the engineering profession*. London: HMSO

Fisher, L. (1976). *Industrial marketing: An analytical approach to planning and execution.* London: Business Books

Ford, D. (1980). 'The development of buyer-seller relationships in industrial markets'. *European Journal of Marketing,* Vol. 14, No. 5/6

Ford, D. (ed.) (1990). *Understanding business markets: Interaction, relationships and networks.* London: Academic Press

Gibney, F. (1975). 'The Japanese and their language'. *Encounter,* No. 44

Glazer, H. Quoted in: Norbury, P. and Bownas, G. (1974)

Gooding, K. (1987). 'An industry squeezed on every side'. *Financial Times,* 30 June

Graham, J.L. (1983). 'Brazilian, Japanese, and American business negotiations'. *Journal of International Business Studies,* Spring/Summer

Graham, J.L. (1985). 'The influence of culture on the process of business negotiations: An exploratory study'. *Journal of International Business Studies,* Spring

Graham, J.L. and Andrews, J.D. (1987). 'A holistic analysis of Japanese and American business negotiations'. *Journal of Business Communication,* Vol. 24, No. 4

Graham, J.L. and Sano, Y. (1984). *Smart bargaining: Doing business with the Japanese.* Mass.: Ballinger

Graham, J.L. and Sano, Y. (1986). 'Across the negotiating table from the Japanese'. *International Marketing Review,* Vol. 3, Autumn

Håkansson, H. (ed.) (1982). *International marketing and purchasing of industrial goods: An interaction approach.* Chichester: John Wiley & Sons

Håkansson, H. and Johanson, J. (1988). 'Formal and informal cooperation strategies in international industrial networks'. In: Contractor, F.J.
and Lorange, P. (eds) *Cooperative strategies in international business.*
Lexington, Mass.: Lexington Books

Håkansson, H., Johanson, J. and Wootz, B. (1976). 'Influence tactics in
buyer-seller processes'. *Industrial Marketing Management,* Vol. 5,
December

Håkansson, H. and Snehota, I. (1990). 'No business is an island: The network concept of business strategy'. *Scandinavian Journal of Management,* Vol. 4, No. 3

Håkansson, H, and Wootz, B. (1975). 'Supplier selection in an international environment'. *Journal of Marketing Research,* Vol. XII, February

Halberstam, D. (1986). *The reckoning.* London: Bantam/Bloomsbury Books

Hallén, L. and Johanson, J. (1985). 'Industrial marketing strategies and
different national environments'. *Journal of Business Research,* Vol. 13

Hallén, L. and Sanderstrom, M. (1989). 'Relationship atmosphere in international business'. Uppsala: University of Uppsala

Hallén, L. and Wiedersheim-Paul, F. (1979). 'Psychic distance and buyer-
seller interaction'. *Organisasjon, Marknad og Samhalle,* Vol. 16, No. 5

Hallén, L. and Wiedersheim-Paul, F. (1984). 'The evolution of psychic dis-
tance in international business relationships'. In: Hagg, I. and
Wiedersheim-Paul, F. (eds) *Between Market and Hierarchy.* Uppsala:
University of Uppsala

Hanson-Abbot, C. (1986). 'Doing business in Japan'. *Management Accounting,* Vol. 64, No. 10

Hardwick, R. and Ford, D. (1986). 'Industrial buyer resources and responsibilities and the buyer-seller relationship'. *Industrial Marketing and
Purchasing,* Vol. 1, No. 3

Harrison, A. and Voss, C (1989). 'Issues in setting up JIT supply', *IJOPM*. 10, 2

Hawrysh, B.M. and Zaikowsky, J.L. (1990). 'Cultural approaches to negotiations: Understanding the Japanese'. *International Marketing Review*, Vol. 7, No. 2

Hijirida, K. and Yoshikawa, M. (1987). *Japanese language and culture for business and travel*. Honolulu: University of Hawaii Press

Holden, N.J. (1983). 'The Japanese language: A partial view from the inside'. *Multilingua*, Vol. 2–3

Holden, N.J. (1988). 'Let's talk business for a change: Negotiating with the Japanese'. *Top Management Digest*, Vol. 1, July

Holden, N.J. (1989). 'Language learning in Japanese corporations: the wider sociolinguistic context'. *Multilingua*. Vol. 9–3

Holden, N.J. (1990). 'Preparing the ground for organisational learning: graduate recruitment programmes in major Japanese corporations. *Management Education and Development*, Vol. 21

Holden, N.J. (1990). 'Internationalisation of Japanese companies: A review of perplexing issues'. Paper presented for the 6th IMP Conference, 7–9 Sept., SDA Bocconi, Milan

Holden, N.J. (1991). 'Japanese buyer-seller relationships: The use of the IMP Interaction Approach to elucidate the distinctively Japanese features'. In: Paliwoda, S. (ed.)

Holding, A.C. (1988). 'The elements of psychic distance in the internationalisation of UK medical equipment manufacturing companies'. Unpublished MSc Dissertation, School of Management, UMIST, Manchester

Horn, M.A., Grubb-Ingram, R. and Masson, R. (1987). 'A Japanese subsidiary in the Scottish electronics industry'. Unpublished paper to the UWIST conference on the Japanization of British industry

Iizuka, Y. and Monden, Y. (1986). 'Mechanism of suppliers' response to the kanban system'. In: Monden, Y. (ed.) *Applying JIT*. Georgia: IEMP

Illidge, R. (1987). 'The management of Japanization: A critical approach'. Unpublished paper to the UWIST conference on the Japanization of British industry

Imai, M. (1986). *Kaizen: The key to Japan's competitive success*. New York: Random House

Japan (Japanese Embassy) No. 485, 27 Feb. (1990)

JETRO (1983). Quoted in: Trevor and Christie, op. cit.

JETRO (1984). 'Japan in Europe: Survey report on management'. Tokyo: JETRO

JETRO (1990). '6th survey report on the current situation of business operations of Japanese manufacturing enterprises in Europe', Tokyo: JETRO

Johanson, J. and Wiedersheim-Paul, F. (1975). 'The internationalisation of the firm – Four Swedish Case studies'. *Journal of Management Studies*, Vol. 12, October

Katzenstein, G. (1990). *Funny business: An outsider's year in Japan*. London: Grafton Books

Keizai Koho Center (1990). *Japan: An international comparison*. Tokyo: Keizai Koho Center

Keizai Koho Center (1991). *Japan: An international comparison*. Tokyo: Keizai Koho Center

Kotler, P., Fahey, L. and Jatuspritak, S. (1986). *The new competition*, Hemel Hempstead: Prentice-Hall

Lu, D. (trs) (1985). 'Kanban-JIT at Toyota'. Cambridge, Mass.: Productivity Press

Macbeth, D.K. and Ferguson, N. (1990). 'Strategic aspects of the supply chain'. Unpublished paper to the OMA/UK conference, Warwick, June

Manthorpe, V. (ed.) (1986). *The Japan diaries of Richard Gordon Smith*, London: Viking

Miller, R.A. (1977). *The Japanese language in contemporary Japan: some sociolinguistic observations*. Washington, D.C.: American Enterprise Institute for Public Policy Research

Miller, R.A. (1982). *Japan's modern myth: the language and beyond*. Tokyo: John Weatherhill

Morgan, J.C. and Morgan, J.J. (1991). *Cracking the Japanese market: Strategies for success in the new global economy*. New York: The Free Press

Morita, A. (1987). *Made in Japan: Akio Morita and Sony*. London: William Collins

Moyle, M. (1985). 'Using joint ventures to enter the Japanese market'. *International Financial Law Review*, November, Vol. 4

Nakane, C. (1973). *Japanese society*, Harmondsworth: Penguin Books

Namiki, N. (1988). 'Japanese trade barriers: How big a problem?' *Business Forum*, Vol. 13

Nash, O. (1938) *I'm a stranger here myself*. Boston: Little, Brown & Co.

NEC (1984). *NEC; The first 80 years*. Tokyo: NEC Corporation

Negishi, T. Quoted in: Trevor, M. and Christie, I. (1988)

Norbury, P. and Bownas, G. (1974). *Business in Japan: A guide to Japanese practice and procedure*. London: Macmillan

Omae, K. (1990). *The borderless world*. London: Fontana

Paliwoda, S. (1991). *New perspectives on research in international marketing*. London: Routledge

Porter, M. (1990). *The competitive advantage of nations.* London: Macmillan

Reischauer, E. (1984). *The Japanese.* Tokyo: Charles E. Tuttle

Rosenberg, L.J. and Thompson, G.J. (1986). 'Deciphering the Japanese cultural code'. International Marketing Review. Vol. 3, Autumn

Sako, M. (1987). 'Supplier relations in Britain: A case of Japanisation'. Unpublished paper to the UWIST conference on the Japanization of British industry

Sansom, G.B. (1950). *The western world and Japan.* London: Cresset Press

Schonberger, R.J. (1982). *Japanese manufacturing techniques.* New York: The Free Press

Schonberger, R.J. (1985). *World class manufacturing.* New York: The Free Press

Seidensticker, E. (1983). *Low city, high city: Tokyo from Edo to the earthquake.* Harmondsworth: Penguin Books

Sheth, J.N. (1973). 'A model of industrial buying behaviour', *Journal of Marketing,* Vol. 37

Shipley, D. (1984). 'Supplier selection criteria for different industrial goods'. *Management Research News,* Vol. 7

Singer, K. (1989). *Mirror, jewel and sword: The geometry of Japanese life.* Tokyo: Kodansha International

Smith, R.G. See: Manthorpe, op. cit.

Storry, R. (1987). *A history of modern Japan.* Harmondsworth: Penguin Books

Street, J. (1925). 'Understanding Japan'. In: Glover, W.J. (ed.). *The Far East: China and Japan.* London: Cassell

Sugimori, Y., Kusuhoni, K., Cho, F. and Uckana, S. (1977). 'Toyota production system and kanban: Materialisation of JIT and respect for human system'. *International Journal of Production Research,* Vol. 15. No. 6

Sullivan, M. (1986). 'How to succeed in the Japanese market'. *FE: The magazine for financial executives,* Vol. 2, Nos. 7–8

Swift, J.S. (1990). *Language as a facet of distance in UK firms interaction with the Spanish market.* Unpublished MSc Dissertation, School of Management, UMIST, Manchester

Tajima, Y. 'Distribution and marketing'. In: Norbury and Bownas, op. cit.

Trevor, M. (1985). *Japanese Industrial Knowledge.* London: Policy Studies Institute

Trevor, M. and Christie, I. (1988). *Manufacturers in Britain and Japan: Competitiveness and the growth of the small firm.* London: Policy Studies Institute

Tsurumi, Y. (1982). 'Managing consumer and industrial marketing systems in Japan'. *Sloan Management Review,* Fall

Tulenko, P. (1987). 'Doing business in Japan'. *Management Decision.* Vol. 25, No. 6

Tung, R. (1984). *Business negotiations with the Japanese.* Lexington, Mass.: Lexington Books

Turnbull, P.J. (1987). 'The limits to Japanisation, JIT and labour, and the UK auto industry'. Unpublished paper to the UWIST conference on the Japanization of British industry

Turnbull, P.W. (1979). 'Roles of personal contacts in industrial export marketing'. *Scandinavian Journal of Management,* 325–337

Turnbull, P.W. (1984). *The reputation and competence of British companies: A European view.* UMIST. Occasional Paper

Turnbull, P.W. and Cunningham, M.T. (1981). *International marketing and purchasing: A survey among marketing and purchasing executives in five European countries.* London: Macmillan

Turnbull, P.W. and Gibbs, M.L. (1987). 'Marketing bank services to corporate consumers: The importance of relationships'. *International Journal of Bank Marketing,* Vol. 14, No. 4

Turnbull, P.W. and Valla, J.-P. (1987). 'Strategic planning in industrial marketing – an interaction approach'. *European Journal of Marketing,* Vol. 121, No. 5

Turnbull, P.W. and Yamada, T. (1984). *The Japanese Approach to Europe.* UMIST Occasional Paper No. 8407

Van Siebold, P.F. (1981; first published in 1841). *Manners and customs of the Japanese in the nineteenth century.* Tokyo: Charles E. Tuttle

Van Wolferen, K. (1989). *The enigma of Japanese power.* London: Macmillan

Van Zandt, H.F. (1970). 'How to negotiate in Japan'. *Harvard Business Review,* November–December

Webster, F.E. and Wind, Y. (1972). *Organizational buying behaviour.* Englewood Cliffs, N.J.: Prentice-Hall

Wilkinson, E. (1983). *Japan versus Europe: A history of misunderstanding.* Harmondsworth: Pelican Books

Wilkinson, E. (1990). *Japan versus the West: Image and reality.* Harmondsworth: Penguin Books

Williamson, O.E. (1979). *Markets and hierarchies: Analysis and antitrust implications.* New York: The Free Press

Zimmerman, M.A. (1985). *Dealing with the Japanese.* London: George Allen & Unwin

Index

KING ALFRED'S COLLEGE LIBRARY

KING ALFRED'S COLLEGE
WINCHESTER

To be returned on or before the day marked
below:-

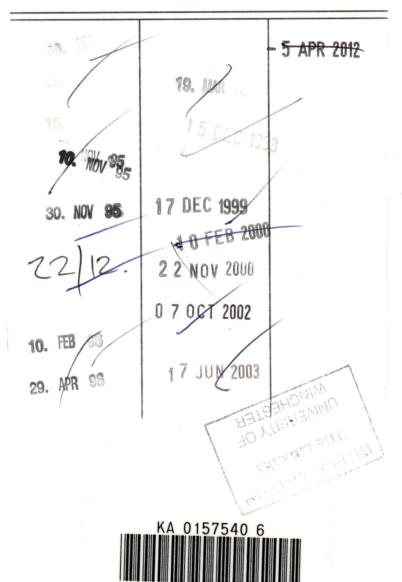

KA 0157540 6